REVISED EDITION

Life in the Slow Lane

W9-CLE-949

FIFTY BACKROAD TOURS OF OHIO

Covered bridges, pioneer cemeteries, Indian memorials, nature preserves, old churches, water mills, and much, much more!

For Denise,
Happy trails!
Jeff Traylor
Nadean DiSabato Traylor

by
JEFF AND NADEAN DISABATO TRAYLOR

Backroad
Chronicles

To Zachary and Jacob
and in memory of Ross Mooney

Life In The Slow Lane is a registered trade name of
Jeffrey and Nadean DiSabato Traylor.

Published and distributed by:

Backroad Chronicles
P.O. Box 292066
Columbus, Ohio 43229

Printed in New Washington, Ohio U.S.A.
by Herald Printing Co., Inc.

ISBN 0-941467-05-8
Fifth Printing

Preface

We are pleased to present this new revised edition of *Life in the Slow Lane: Fifty Backroad Tours of Ohio.* All fifty tours that appeared in the former edition have been personally checked and updated. New historical information that has come to light since the former edition was published has been included. Some route changes have been made due to changes in road conditions. In some cases, tours have been deleted due to significant changes that have taken place along the route, including urban encroachment.

The deletion of eight original tours presented us with the opportunity to expand the book into the hill country of Ohio. Eight new tours of these scenic hills are included in this volume for the first time, featuring the mysterious mounds, distinctive canal locks, log cabin shrines, old mills, charcoal iron furnaces, and, yes, covered bridges that huddle in the misty valleys of Ohio's hill country. We invite the reader to visit Ohio's prairie remnants and virgin forests that survive to this day; see the monuments to great Indian chiefs who struggled to save their way of life; marvel at the workmanship and ingenuity of the early pioneers and builders of Ohio; and be refreshed and renewed by the natural beauty of our state.

We wish you many happy and joyful days on Ohio's back roads. We hope you have as much fun as we did!

Jeff and Nadean Traylor

Introduction

This tourbook was written for modern day adventurers who wish to travel the backroads to Ohio's past and discover a world that lies beyond the freeways and city lights. Whether you are a weekend wanderer or armchair explorer, Sunday driver or touring bicyclist, you will find many hours of enjoyable and informative touring on these country roads. Ohio's past becomes present as you discover covered bridges, Indian memorials, pioneer cemeteries, water mills, old churches, and other historical points of interest. Our natural heritage likewise is awaiting your exploration in the prairies, woodlands, islands and lakes of Ohio. To further complement your ramblings, many of the loops also include swimming beaches, campgrounds, picnic areas, and walking trails.

A simple-to-use trip planning guide provides information to help you select your tour, and an Ohio outline map gives you the loop's location at a glance. A historical narrative accompanies each loop description, and information about the various points of interest is provided. Several points of interest, such as round barns or old mills, are on private property, but are clearly visible from the road as you pass by. County road maps have been used as base maps for these self-guided tours, and each map is clearly marked and annotated. Routes have been selected that offer the best combination of scenery, surface, and low traffic, while connecting the points of interest. Of course, road and traffic conditions are subject to change. Because bicyclists and motorists must share the roads, we urge cyclists and drivers alike to observe safe riding/driving practices, and for cyclists especially to know their skills and physical limits before embarking on their bicycles. The authors assume no responsibility for the safety of persons using these routes.

Food and drink are frequently, but not always, available along the routes, therefore we find it good practice to carry water and sandwiches—especially when we find a scenic picnic spot! And one final word about country roads—they sometimes have several names, but the road number is usually reliable. When in doubt, counting crossroads and using the map scale are useful tools for the backroad explorer. But if all else fails and you stray from the route, keep your eyes open. There's no telling what you may discover!

HAPPY TRAILS!

About the Authors

Ohio natives Jeffrey and Nadean DiSabato Traylor are devoted explorers of out-of-the-way places, and spent six years researching, exploring and writing *Life In The Slow Lane*. In addition to being a writer, Jeff holds a graduate degree from The Ohio State University and a professional counseling license. Nadean attended The Ohio State University, and has a professional background in the field of mental retardation. Her interests include pioneer crafts and raising chickens. Prior to embarking on *Life In The Slow Lane*, the Traylors owned and operated a retail business in Columbus' historic North Market.

Acknowledgments

The authors wish to thank the following agencies for providing information that helped make this book possible:

The Ohio Historical Society

The Ohio Department of Natural Resources

The Ohio Department of Transportation

and numerous libraries, museums, and historical societies throughout Ohio. We are also indebted to many individuals who have contributed to this project in a variety of ways, including Steve Gordon, Barb Padgett, Vern Pack, Paul and Rita Bishop, John and Ellen Schwab, Dick Helwig, Dr. Sal Lowry, Jane Willman, Marcus Orr, Joe and Pat Toronto, Jeff Reed, Tom and Norma Traylor, Seth B. Schlotterbeck, Jim Turner, Joanne Kuhn, Mike Bristle, Julie Tkach Hesse, and the many people we met along the road who welcomed us and shared their knowledge. Thank you one and all.

Abbreviation Key

The following road number prefixes will be encountered occasionally throughout the book: T or TR = Township Road; C, CR, or no prefix on map = County Road; SR or Ohio Outline = State Route. Extra caution is advised in those few instances where it is necessary to cross or travel a short distance along a state route.

Contents

SECTION I. *Central Ohio*

Trip Planning Guide
Central Ohio

# Name	Length (miles)	Historical site	Nature preserve	Museum	Covered bridge (#)	Scenic river	Swimming	Picnic tables	Camping (State Park)	Pioneer cemetery	Hiking/walking trails
1. Pioneer Pilgrimage	36		X		2	X				X	
2. Marion Meander	40		X							X	
*3. Ice Age Deja Vu	39		X				X	X	X	X	X
*4. Mackachack	39	X	X				X	X	X	X	X
5. Treaty Line	49	X				X	X	X		X	
6. Books of Stone	40	X			1		X	X	X	X	
*7. Slate Run Farm	30		X	X				X	X		X
*8. The Logan Elm	29	X						X	X		
9. Glacier's Edge	34		X		1					X	X
10. Flint Ridge	20	X	X	X				X			X

* Camp-Over Option: <u>Two</u> loops leave from same state park where camping is available.

Tour Loop Locations
Central Ohio

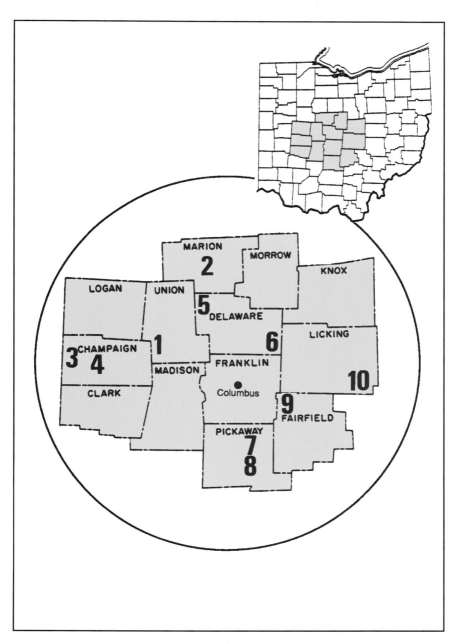

LOOP #1

Length: 36 miles

Terrain: Flat

County: Union/Madison

Pioneer Pilgrimage

This enchanting tour through the flat farmland of Union and Madison Counties meanders along the scenic Big Darby Creek, where muskrats and turtles swim beneath covered bridges as red-tailed hawks circle lazily overhead, indigo buntings flit along fencerows while kestrels, those proctors of the power lines, cast watchful eyes on the proceedings below. Historic cemeteries, where Ohio's early pioneers now rest, and remnants of the "Darby Plains", the sea of waving grasses and brilliant prairie flowers that greeted these early settlers, round out this pilgrimage into Ohio's pioneer past.

As you ride through these Darby Plains, cast your imagination back about 175 years, and visualize an area vastly different from what you see today. Put yourself into the shoes of Charles and Alvira Andrews, one of the first families to settle here in "The Barrens", as these Darby Plains were then called. Moving into this area in 1814, the Andrews' were not settling rich farmland, but rather moving into an almost worthless extensive wet prairie, quite similar to the tall grass prairies of the west. The dense prairie grass grew to a height of eight feet, and the poorly drained land was covered with water most of the year. But as is characteristic of prairies, the land became dry in the fall and subject to raging prairie fires, a device that protects the succession of prairie plants but endangers people and slows settlement. The whole area was described as a sea of prairie grasses and colorful prairie wildflowers.

A few years after the arrival of the Andrews', their five-year old daughter, Almira, became ill and died, and was the first person laid to rest in what is now called Smith Cemetery. Other family members joined her as the years went by, until in 1834 the land was transferred to the Darby Township trustees, and the original owners left the plains for good.

The original vast prairie has all but disappeared, except for some scatterings of burr oak trees and a few patches of prairie plants. Appropriately enough, one of the best remnants of the prairie is found at Smith Cemetery, where the settlers now rest in the same prairie soil they settled. This sod still supports relics of the original prairie plant life with its beautiful prairie wildflowers. The Ohio Department of Natural Resources manages this plot to perpetuate the prairie flora and preserve the historic tombstones, which are hidden in the prairie grasses.

Thirty species of native prairie plants have been identified in Smith Cemetery, and a checklist of some of these is provided here. Take along your wildflower book and a sack lunch for this ride, and see how many of these beautiful prairie plants you can identify. The peak blooming time for these wildflowers is late June through most of August.

Two covered bridges along the loop stand as monuments to Ohio-builder Reuben Partridge. Reuben was born in 1823, and at the age of twelve, moved to Union County with his mother and attended a log schoolhouse in Marysville. He went on to learn wagon and carriage making, but his true love was covered bridge building. While yet a young man, he developed a better, stronger design, which he patented as his "high truss bridge improvement". Mr. Partridge built nearly 200 bridges in Union and adjoining counties, including the two covered bridges on this loop. He continued building bridges into his later years, until one day in 1900, at the age of 77, he fell through the timbers of a bridge he was erecting over Blues Creek and was fatally injured. These bridges stand today as fitting monuments to kindly old Reuben Partridge, an Ohio-builder who gave his life to his profession.

POINTS OF INTEREST:

1. *Milford Center, Ohio*
   The ride begins in this little village, and a parking lot is located near the center of town by the Big Darby Creek. Leave town via W. State St.

2. *Little Darby Covered Bridge*
   This beautiful bridge, still in use today, was built by Reuben Partridge, probably in 1877.

5

3. **Bigelow Prairie Preserve**
Prairie wildflowers still bloom mid to late summer in this original prairie sod.

4. **May Flag Farm Log Cabin**
This wonderful example of an early log home from the settlement days is on private properly, but is visible from the road as you pass by.

5. **Smith Cemetery Prairie Preserve**
Another remnant of the original "Darby Plains", this small pre-serve is found one-half mile after your turn onto Boyd Road. An opening in a farm field leads back about 75 yards to the pre-serve. Both the Bigelow and Smith Preserves are maintained by the Ohio Department of Natural Resources.

6. **Reed Covered Bridge**
Contrary to the sign, this bridge was probably built by Reuben Partridge in 1884. (Update: Bridge collapsed in 1993.)

7. **Robinson-Mitchell Pioneer Cemetery**
Located just north of the covered bridge, this historic cemetery is said to be the location of an even earlier Indian burying ground. Memorials to the Mitchell and Robinson pioneer families are found here, as well as Mary Hawn's marker that reads "First White Female Child Born in Ohio".

8. **Woods Pioneer Cemetery**
Rev. Samuel Woods settled on the Big Darby in 1806 and be-came a noted preacher at an early age. In 1808 he served as the first minister at the Presbyterian Church in Milford Center, a post he held until his death in 1815. His marker is among the few in this overgrown cemetery, the oldest in the township.

Prairie Plant Checklist

☐ Wild Garlic

☐ Big Bluestem

☐ Little Bluestem

☐ Canadian Anemone

☐ Smooth Aster

☐ New Jersey Tea

☐ Gray Dogwood

☐ Purple Coneflower

☐ Gray Willow

☐ Whorled Rosinweed

☐ Stiff Goldenrod

☐ Indian Grass

☐ Flowering Spurge

☐ Biennial Guara

☐ Ox-Eye

☐ Prairie False Indigo

☐ Wild Bergamot

☐ Virginia Mountain Mint

☐ Gray-Headed Coneflower

☐ Black-Eyed Susan

☐ Prairie Cord Grass

☐ Skunk Meadow-Rue

☐ Golden Alexanders

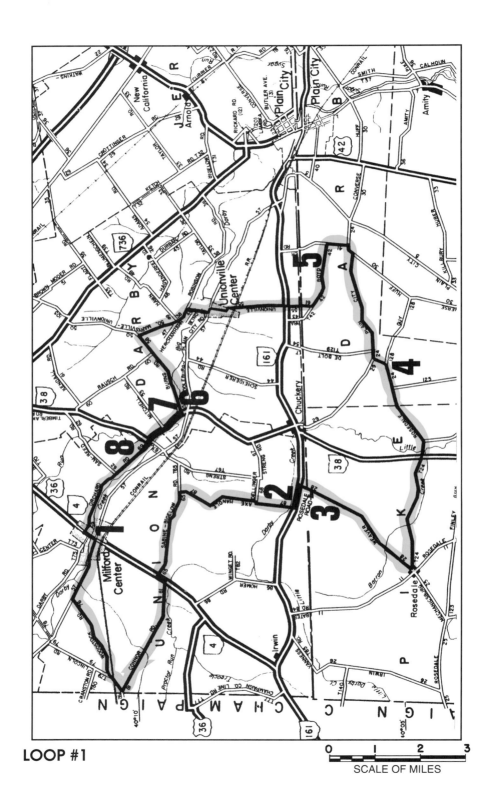

LOOP #1

SCALE OF MILES

0   1   2   3

LOOP #2

Length: 40 miles

Terrain: Flat

County: Marion

A Marion Meander

This tour through the countryside of Marion County wends its way to a prairie preserve with beautiful wildflowers, passes old one-room schoolhouses, crosses ornate bridges, and side-tracks to Old Man Grimm's Grave, one of the most peculiar in Ohio.

It oftentimes seems that what cannot be done by design is achieved by accident, and the saving of Claridon Prairie, a piece of the original Sandusky Plains, is such an example. While virtually every acre of the once vast prairie has been cut by the plow and turned into a bounty of corn and soybeans, a narrow mile-long strip of original prairie sod survives yet today at the northern end of this loop. This "flower bed" of prairie plants was saved when the road and railway were constructed side by side, and now it provides us with its own bounty of 75 species of grasses and flowers, most of which bloom mid to late summer. A historical marker for the Claridon Prairie is located at the west end of the strip.

The Claridon Prairie is not the only unusual feature found along this route. The traveler who wishes to make a short side-trip east on Cardington Road will discover a small sandstone "pen" right along the road. Here lies John Grimm, who died of blood poisoning in 1833 after a tree he was cutting fell on him. When the road was straightened, other graves were moved, but John's relatives from Cleveland put up this sandstone box around the marker, leaving him right beside the road—and, you guessed it, beneath a large tree!

The route crosses several early metal bridges as it meanders along the "Olentangy" River, a river whose name is subject to some controversy. The Indian name for the river was "Keenhongsheconsepung", meaning "tool sharpening river", or, in English, the Whetstone River. In 1833, the Ohio Legislature mistakenly called this the Olentangy, giving the name Whetstone to another stream in nearby Morrow County. While most Buckeyes know the river here as the Olentangy, many proud

Marion Countians still refer to it by its "right" name of Whetstone, as evidenced by the name of the road that follows its course.

POINTS OF INTEREST:

1. *Waldo, Ohio*
   The tour begins in the village of Waldo. Fried bologna connoisseurs know Waldo as the home of the G&R Grille, the local tavern that serves the world-famous G&R bologna sandwich Monday-Saturday.

2. *One Room Schoolhouse*
   This former schoolhouse now serves as a storage building on private property.

3. *Claridon Prairie*
   "Prairie dogs" who wish to explore the prairie flowers will find a checklist in Loop #1.

4. *Plotner Pioneer Cemetery*
   Ebenezer Lewis, Revolutionary War veteran, is buried in this old cemetery.

5. *1915 Metal Bridge*
   Although several early iron bridges are found along this loop, this one stands out because of its ornate beauty.

6. *Richland Township House*
   This 1888 schoolhouse has been saved from ruin by its present use as the township hall.

7. *Old Man Grimm's Grave*

8. *Smith Cemetery*
   Israel Clark, Revolutionary War veteran and early pioneer, is buried here with other early settlers. A marker for Joseph Powell claims he was a Revolutionary War veteran who died at the age of 101, a claim that has been disputed.

9. *Old St. James Church*
   Now the home of the Whetstone Grange, this old church building was one of the earliest in the county.

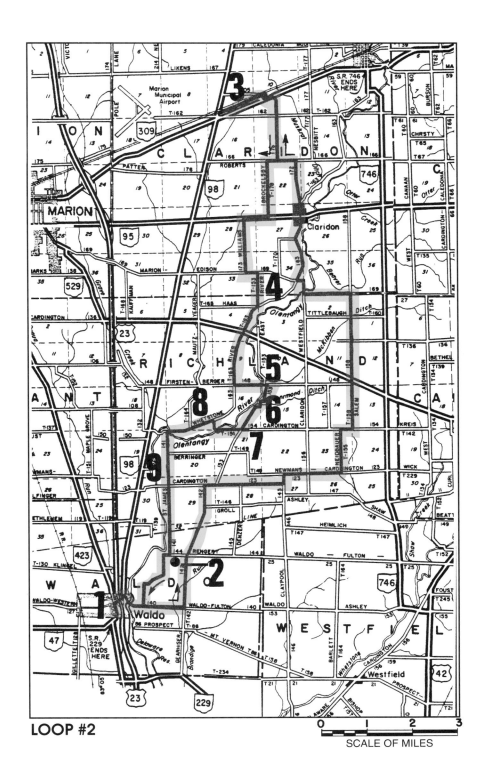

LOOP #2

SCALE OF MILES

0   1   2   3

LOOP #3

Length: 39 miles

Terrain: Flat to gently rolling

County: Champaign

Ice Age Deja Vu

As is typical of the landscape in the till plains of western Central Ohio, this tour takes you over flat to gently rolling countryside, along back roads through broad valleys and open farmland. You may wish to couple this tour with the Mackachack Tour and a campout, as both trips leave from Kiser Lake State Park.

Ohio has played host to a number of guests who came from the north during the Ice Age thousands of years ago, and stayed on after the glacier retreated. This makes it possible for us today to visit these guests, the plants and trees of the north, right in our own backyard. Of course, these trees and plants typical of the northern forests require very special conditions that are not readily found this far south in North America. Fortunately, a cold spring flowing through glacial outwash provides the necessary environment for these northern Michigan and Canadian plants at Cedar Bog. In addition to the northern plants, many prairie plants can also be found here. An unusual stand of arbor vitae, or white cedar, is present in the bog, and another stand this large won't be found without traveling far to the north.

The bog has a characteristic accumulation of peat formed by non-decaying plant material in the oxygen-starved water, and certain places in the bog may quake from this mass of peat being supported on shallow, high volume springs. Therefore, a floating boardwalk is provided to lead you through the bog. Take along your wildflower book to identify the many species found here, or just enjoy a stroll. A checklist of some of the plants you may find here is provided on the next page. If you are visiting during mosquito season, remember to bring your repellent.

POINTS OF INTEREST:

1. *Kiser Lake State Park*
   The park has a swimming beach, picnic tables, hiking trails, and camping.

2. *Nettle Creek Pioneer Cemetery*
   This cemetery has stones dating back to 1818, and veterans of the Revolutionary and Civil Wars are buried here. Several unusual markers fashioned as tree trunks can be found here.

3. *Cedar Bog Nature Preserve*
   Operated and maintained by the Ohio Historical Society, the bog is open for public tours April to September, Saturdays and Sundays at 1:00 and 3:00 P.M. Admission fee.

4. *Prince Pioneer Cemetery*
   This small hilltop cemetery has stones dating back to 1834.

5. *Round Barn*
   The rarest of barns, this circular gem greets you at the edge of St. Paris.

Cedar Bog Plant Checklist

MARL MEADOW:

- ☐ Calopogon Orchid
- ☐ False Asphodel
- ☐ Bunchflower
- ☐ Marsh Violet
- ☐ Kalm's Lobelia
- ☐ Grass-of-Parnassus
- ☐ Tuberous Indian Plantain
- ☐ Chara
- ☐ Cotton Grass
- ☐ Round-Leaf Sundew
- ☐ Ohio Goldenrod
- ☐ Riddell's Goldenrod
- ☐ Purple Gerardia
- ☐ Ladies-Tresses Orchid
- ☐ Fringed Gentian

FEN MEADOW:

- ☐ Shrubby Cinquefoil
- ☐ Alder Buckthorn
- ☐ Swamp Birch
- ☐ Ninebark
- ☐ Poison Sumac
- ☐ Alder
- ☐ Nannyberry

FEN MEADOW WILDFLOWERS:

- ☐ Canada Mayflower
- ☐ Starflower
- ☐ Pink Lady's Slipper
- ☐ Yellow Lady's Slipper
- ☐ New England Aster

SHRUB MEADOW ZONE:

- ☐ Arbor Vitae (White Cedar)
- ☐ Tamarack

PRAIRIE SPECIES:

- ☐ Indian Grass
- ☐ Prairie Cordgrass
- ☐ Big Bluestem
- ☐ Queen-of-the-Prairie
- ☐ Nodding Wild Onion
- ☐ Prairie Dock
- ☐ Spiked Blazing Star
- ☐ Sneezeweed

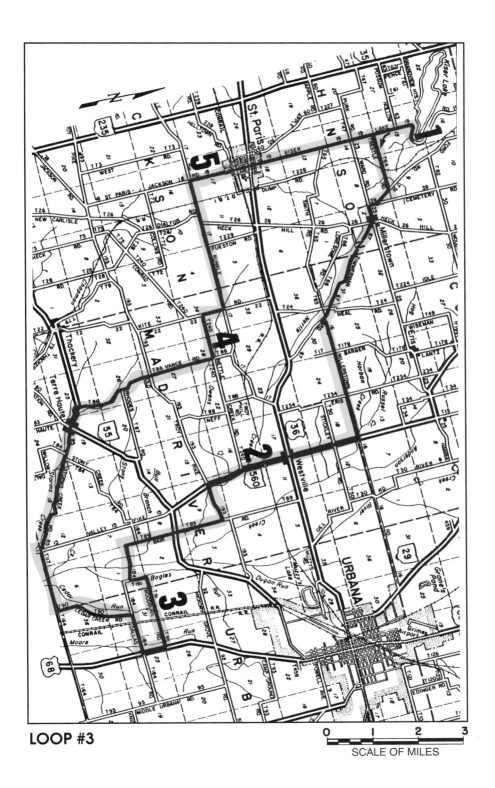

LOOP #3

0   1   2   3
SCALE OF MILES

LOOP #4

Length: 39 miles

Terrain: Flat to gently rolling

County: Champaign/Logan

The Mackachack Tour

Diversity is the hallmark of this 39 mile loop, one of two to begin at Kiser Lake State Park, where camping is available. Castles and caverns, log cabins, pioneer cemeteries, and cascading creeks are all part of this loop through historic Champaign county. In the fall, migrating Canada geese can be seen on the ponds that dot the gently rolling countryside as you travel these quiet back lanes. But were you to travel back in time exactly two centuries ago, you would have been in a time of turmoil and conflict on this very ground known to the Indians as Mackachack, or "Smiling Valley".

All that is left of Mackachack Town now is a small roadside marker that hints at the events of the 1780's. At this site, in October of 1786, an officer of General Benjamin Logan's army, Major Simon Kenton, watched from cover as a deserter from the troops warned the Indians of an impending attack from the army; he also saw the Shawnees kill the deserter on the spot after giving them the warning, for they had no respect for one who would betray his own people. Kenton returned to General Logan with word of the betrayal, and it was decided that they would join forces with Colonel Daniel Boone and attack the villages as soon as possible. When the attack came the next morning, only a few warriors were in the village, and it wasn't much of a skirmish. Chief Moluntha, aged King of the Shawnees, was captured, and after being promised protection by General Logan, was slain by a deranged army captain, who was in turn assaulted by his own troops and later court-martialed. The army went on to destroy eight Indian towns located in the Mackachack area.

This wasn't the first time that strife, or Simon Kenton, had come to Mackachack. Eight years previous, in 1778, Kenton had been captured by the Shawnees, far to the south of Mackachack. Due to his great fame among the Indians as the greatest fighter and frontiersman alive, he was sentenced to die in a most grueling and public way. He was marched from Indian town to Indian town, from Chalagatha to Mackachack, nine towns in all, and forced to run a gauntlet each time. Miraculously, he was able to escape death time after time, until he was "rescued" by British soldiers who wanted to interrogate him at Detroit. The Shawnees came to believe that Simon Kenton must have been under the protection of the Great Spirit and therefore was not to be harmed. And, indeed, Simon Kenton eventually died in his bed in nearby Urbana at the age of eighty-eight.

Mackachack Town is gone, but the Smiling Valley remains with a large number of interesting historical and natural sites that provide a full day of exploring for the modern adventurer.

POINTS OF INTEREST:

1. **Kiser Lake State Park**
   The park has a swimming beach, picnic tables, hiking trails, and camping.

2. **Mackachack Town Historical Marker**

3. **Castle Piatt Mac-A-Cheek**
   Built by General Abram Sanders Piatt in 1864 in the Norman-French chateau style, the castle contains furnishings up to 250 years old. The castle is open daily Spring to Fall, admission charge.

   Piatt Log Home
   This newly restored log home located just south of the castle was originally built in 1828 by federal Judge Benjamin Piatt. When the judge was away from home, the cabin served as a station on the underground railroad under the auspices of Piatt's wife, Elizabeth, an ardent abolitionist. The home is now open to the public, and houses a gift and antique shop. Open Monday-Saturday 11-5, Sunday 1-5, May-December.

   Piatt Cemetery
   Located a short distance south of the log home on a hilltop, this old cemetery has stones dating back to 1808.

4. **Mac-O-Chee Castle**
   This striking 1879 stone castle was the home of Col. Donn Piatt. Open daily in summer. Admission charge.

5. **Ohio Caverns**

   These are the largest and perhaps most colorful caverns in the state, and boast the Crystal King, the largest crystal white stalactite in Ohio. Open year round, admission charge includes a guided tour.

6. **Century Old Meeting House**

   Built in 1881, the Mt. Tabor Church Building is the century old meeting house. The old cemetery on the south side of the church has stones dating back to 1817, and gravestones of veterans of the Revolutionary War, War of 1812, and the Civil War are found here.

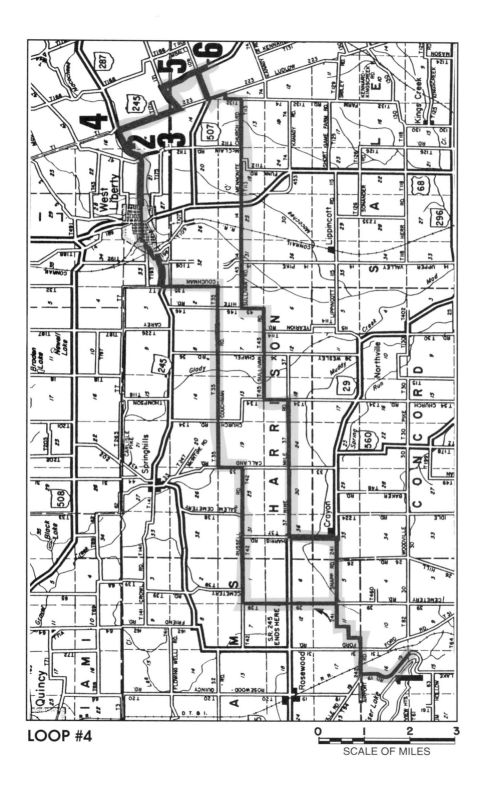

LOOP #4

0   1   2   3

SCALE OF MILES

LOOP #5

Length: 49 miles

Terrain: Flat with a few small hills at the beginning

County: Delaware/Marion/Union

Treaty Line Tour

This tour has long been one of our favorites, and we have enjoyed it in all seasons. It is a very flat loop with almost no traffic, and in some places these country lanes are no wider than drive-ways. The tour winds along a scenic stretch of the Scioto River before heading into open farmland. Birdlife is abundant along the river, and includes red-headed woodpeckers, kingfishers, bluebirds, flickers, ducks, geese, and more. Turtles can be seen sunning themselves on rocks in the summertime. Farm animals abound in the countryside, with cows grazing in the pastures and horses frolicking in the corrals.

In addition to being a beautiful trip through the countryside, the tour passes through an area of historic significance. Had you taken this tour in 1795, you would have stayed within the territory of the United States government, but just barely! Ohio was then part of the Northwest Territory, and General "Mad" Anthony Wayne had just defeated the Indians and supposedly secured the area for settlement. The treaty signed in Greenville in 1795 designated land north of the Treaty Line as Indian territory, with land south of the line to be open for settlement. This tour goes only as far north as the Greenville Treaty Line (now called Boundary Road), turns and follows it westward for a few miles, then loops southward toward Richwood. The journey touches, but does not enter, the former Indian Territory. Along the way, the keen-eyed "scout" will spot some old cemeteries, one-room schoolhouses, an interesting wooden foot bridge, the oldest church in Delaware County, and several steel truss bridges built around the turn of this century. For the botanically inclined, one of the few stands of white cedar found in Ohio can be seen at the confluence of Mills Creek and the Scioto River.

POINTS OF INTEREST:

1. **Ostrander, Ohio**
   The ride begins in the village of Ostrander.

2. **1914 Steel Truss Bridge over Mill Creek**

3. **Mills Road Foot Bridge**
   This old abandoned foot bridge spans Mill Creek, but is now closed to foot traffic.

4. **Route Note:** Cyclists can make a left turn from Mills Road onto S.R. 257, then a quick right onto Bellpoint Road and across the abandoned bridge over the Scioto River. This bridge is closed to automobile traffic, so if you are driving, turn right from Mills Road onto Rt. 257, then left onto Rt. 42 to cross the river.

5. **The Old Stone Church**
   This historic landmark was built in 1835 of gray limestone. It has been in worship for over 150 years, making it the oldest church in continuous service in Delaware County.

6. **Prospect, Ohio**
   Cross the beautiful 1913 steel bridge that spans the Scioto River here, then turn right at the end of the bridge. You'll pass by the cemetery and 1884 school bell as you leave town.

7. **Greenville Treaty Line Marker**

8. **Brown-Tyler Pioneer Cemetery**
   This small cemetery has stones pre-dating the Civil War by twenty years. The graves of Civil War veterans are marked as such.

9. **One Room School and Cemetery**

10. **Richwood Park**
    This community park has a swimming area, picnic tables, and a shelterhouse. Food and drink are available in the town. Leave Richwood via E. Ottawa Street.

11. **Steel Truss Bridge over Bokes Creek**

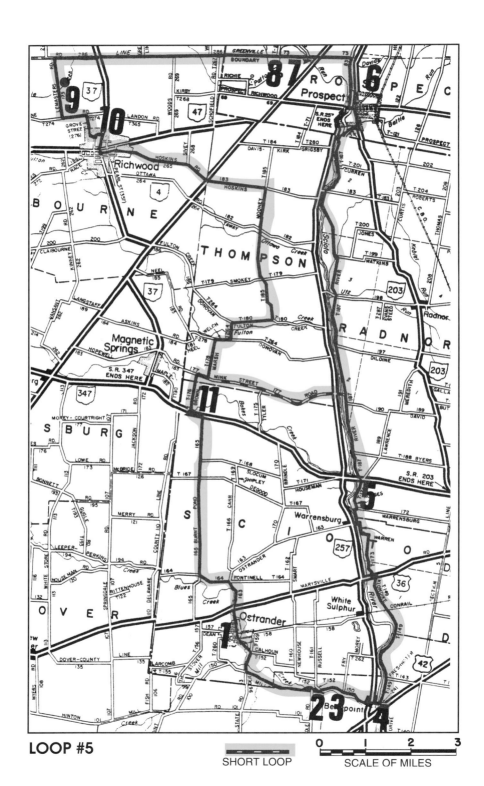

LOOP #5

SHORT LOOP

0   1   2   3

SCALE OF MILES

LOOP #6

Length: 40 miles

Terrain: Flat

County: Delaware

Books of Stone

This 40 mile tour from Alum Creek State Park leads through level open farmland, passes by the last covered bridge in Delaware County, and visits three of those history books of stone, the pioneer cemetery.

There are thousands of small pioneer cemeteries scattered throughout Ohio, many with only a handful of graves. These cemeteries tell the story of our state, its settlers, and in large part reflect the history of the new United States. The fact that the earliest cemeteries date back only to the early 1800's is testament to the youthfulness of Ohio, which saw the land opened for settlement after the Greenville Treaty of 1795. Only eight years later, Ohio became the seventeenth state of the Union, and the first state carved from the Northwest Territory. You can trace the history of our nation's early conflicts with a walk through these cemeteries, as the stones mark the final resting place of the soldiers who fought for the principles of the Declaration of Independence in the Revolutionary War; who defended the new country against the British and the Indians of Tecumseh's federation in the War of 1812; and the tragic war that pitted brother against brother, the Civil War, fifty years later. Proportionate to her population, Ohio sent more of her sons to the Union Army than any other state. The stones also tell the story of the migration into Ohio, as settlers poured in from Connecticut, Virginia, Kentucky, and Pennsylvania seeking the freedom and promise of the new land.

History is found not only on the stones, but in the size and location of the cemeteries themselves, as they parallel the development of Ohio. The earliest cemeteries are usually small family plots, with only a handful of graves, located on a piece of high ground on the homestead. In death, as in life, the small group of stones symbolizes the family huddled against a hostile new environment, drawing on itself for support. A short time later, as small communities grew, the church lot became the cemetery for a larger number of families. Eventually, the cemeteries outgrew the church lots, and were located on the outskirts of town, "out of sight, out of mind", according to some.

The artwork and inscriptions on the stones reveal the themes of the ages. Many offer religious inscriptions, with open books and fingers pointing toward heaven; others chastise the living and warn them that "as I am now, so you will be". The willow tree, a symbol of sorrow, adorns many of the earliest stones. The evolution of the material for the markers is also clearly evident, with sandstone being used for the earliest gravestones. Sandstone gave a brown, red, or beige appearance, and its coarse grain made it difficult to inscribe deeply. Therefore, many of these early stones have weathered poorly and are now illegible. White marble or Lithopolis freestone came into use around 1850, and the tablet markers gave way in the 1870's to varied shapes such as tree trunks, pillars, obelisks, and other forms.

The old pioneer cemeteries, although engraved in stone, are a vanishing record of history. Each year, the old stones become more weathered, and more become illegible; some cemeteries disappear altogether, as their stones are broken or lost. But for now, these history books of stone are there for the reading.

POINTS OF INTEREST:

1. *Alum Creek State Park*
   This park offers swimming, picnicking, and camping.

2. *Africa Cemetery*
   This cemetery was relocated to this site upon construction of the nearby dam. Many of the early markers, dating back to 1823, have been restored to legibility.

3. *Old Eden-Old Kilbourne Pioneer Cemetery*
   This cemetery has stones dating back to at least 1832.

4. *Chambers Covered Bridge*
   Built in 1874, this is the only remaining covered bridge in Delaware County. It was built by Everett Sherman, who later moved to Preble County, Ohio and built more bridges there.

5. *Old Blue Church Cemetery*
   The old church is gone, but the cemetery remains. Stones date back to 1824, and include soldiers of the Revolution, War of 1812, and Civil War. The church bell, cast in 1850, is preserved at the site.

6. *General Rosecrans Historical Marker*
   This stone marks the birthplace of General William Rosecrans, Civil War hero. His burial in Arlington National Cemetery was attended by President Theodore Roosevelt, the Cabinet, and generals from both the Union and Confederate Armies. Rosecrans was part of the remarkable 23rd Ohio Regiment, from which also came a U.S. Supreme Court Justice and two presidents, Rutherford B. Hayes and William McKinley.

7. *Africa, Ohio*
   Settled by William Patterson in 1824, this town was originally named East Orange. A famous stop on the Underground Railroad, the town became known as Africa due to the large number of freed slaves who settled here after the Civil War. The town has now all but disappeared.

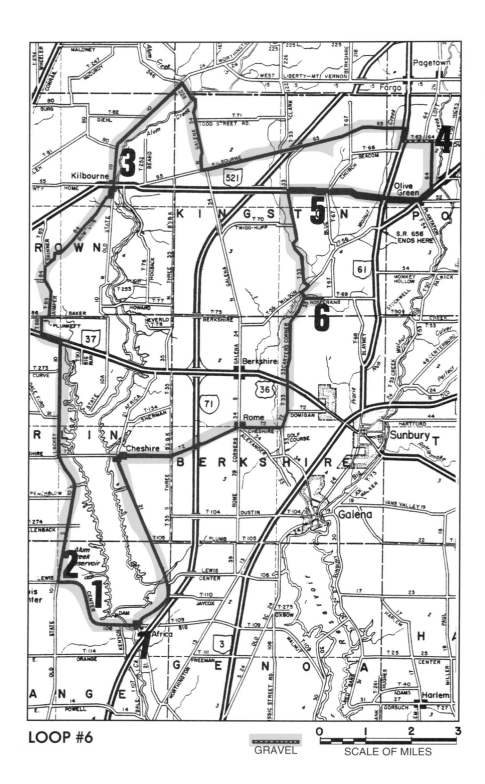

LOOP #6

GRAVEL

SCALE OF MILES

0 1 2 3

LOOP #7

Length: 30 miles

Terrain: Mostly flat with a few small hills

County: Pickaway

Slate Run Farm

The Slate Run Farm Tour, like the Logan Elm Tour, leaves from A.W. Marion State Park, where camping is available. The Slate Run Farm Tour is a 30 mile loop rich in the history of the land and the people who farmed it a century ago. As you ride the ridge top northward, you'll look out over productive farmland and observe modern agriculture at work. Trucks, tractors, combines, and other modern equipment make it possible to farm a much larger area than was dreamed of a century ago. This is a ride of contrasts, because you are traveling back in time to the 1880's, to a farm where the tractors are huge draught horses and the trucks are horse drawn wagons.

Slate Run Living Historical Farm is not an ordinary farm, but rather an actual working farm using the methods and tools of the 1880's. The farm house was built in 1856 and is still furnished accordingly, and the large red barn was built in 1880. The activities of the farm are always changing, as are the natural rhythms of the seasons and weather. You may see the men and women, in period dress, making soap, butchering, getting the hay in, or tending the farm animals among the myriad chores to be performed.

From observing people at Slate Run Farm, we go to observing wildlife at Stage's Pond, one of the best spots in the area for observing migrating waterfowl in the spring and fall. Seventeen thousand years ago the glacier covering this area began to recede, and a huge ice chunk broke off and was left behind. The stranded "iceberg" became covered with sand and gravel pouring off the retreating glacier, and when this chunk finally melted after perhaps a millenium, it left a 64 acre depression in the earth. About half of the depression is underwater and forms the kettle lake called Stage's Pond. In addition to the migrating waterfowl that visit the pond, summer residents include great blue herons and other shorebirds. Nearby wooded areas and open

27

fields support songbirds, quail, pheasant, and hawks. A wide variety of wildflowers can be found here from April through October, with the spring being the peak time for color and variety.

POINTS OF INTEREST:

1. *A. W. Marion State Park*
   This park has a 160 acre lake, hiking trails, picnicking, and camping.

2. *Slate Run Living Historical Farm*
   The farm is open daily in the summer except Monday; after Labor Day closed Monday and Tuesday. Operated by the Metropolitan Park District of Columbus and Franklin County, there is an admission charge.

3. *Ashville Heritage Museum*
   This little museum is a very friendly and interesting place. The world's first traffic light, which hung in Ashville until only a few years ago, is on display here. The museum is located at 24 Long Street, just one block off the loop in town. Hours: 1-3 Tuesday through Friday, 10-3 Saturday, Apr.-Nov. Donations accepted .

4. *Stage's Pond Nature Preserve*
   Open year round, dawn to dusk. Water, latrines, an observation blind, and walking trails are provided here.

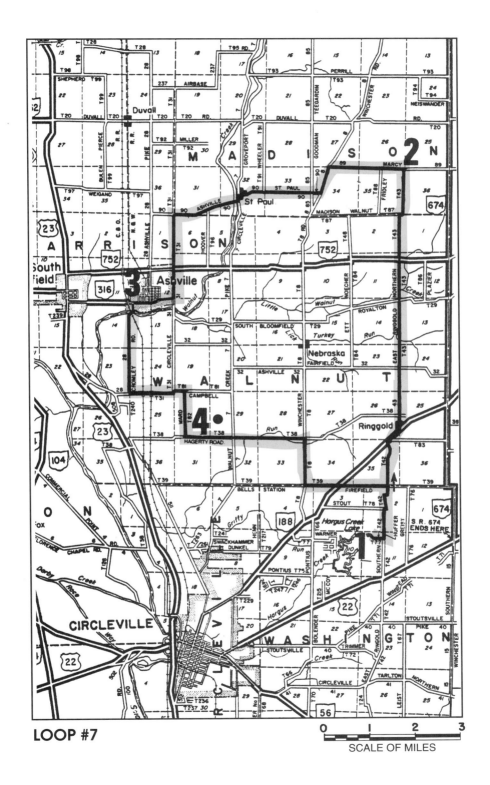

LOOP #7

SCALE OF MILES

0   1   2   3

LOOP #8

Length: 29 miles

Terrain: Rolling

County: Pickaway

The Logan Elm

This tour, as well as the Slate Run Farm Tour, begins at A.W. Marion State Park near Circleville, providing the opportunity to couple two days of touring with a campout at the park. The route takes you over rolling hills, through beautiful countryside, and offers panoramic views overlooking pastures, ponds, and barns. The site of the Logan Elm, now a state historical site, is the highlight of this trip. This important memorial is located on the Pickaway Plains, an area steeped in history, and commemorates one of the darkest pages in Ohio's past.

The recorded history of Pickaway County began in 1774 when Lord Dunmore led an army into the Ohio Valley to wage war against the Indians. Shawnee leaders tried to persuade the Mingo chief, Tay-ga-yee-ta, known as Logan on the frontier, to join them in battling the militia. Chief Logan, however, was a man of peace, known to the Indians and whites alike as a warm and friendly person. He had, in fact, served as a peacemaker in previous conflicts, including the French and Indian War. He was welcomed in various tribal houses and settlers' homes, for he was considered most trustworthy. As one grizzled old frontiersman said, "Logan is the best specimen of humanity I ever met with, either white or red." Logan refused the pleas of the Shawnees to take up arms against Dunmore, counseling instead for peace and negotiation. But only a few weeks later, while Logan was away, his family was viciously murdered by a party of men led by Jacob Greathouse, who posed as friends and lured the Indians into their camp for games and drink. Upon finding his family murdered, the chief no longer sought peace, but rather sought revenge. When the fighting ended, General Dunmore had won the war, but Logan refused to join the other Indian leaders at the treaty signing with the general. Instead, he dictated a message beneath a spreading elm tree to be read for him at the meeting. Although he mistakenly accused Colonel Cresap for his family's murder, the

30

speech is one of the most eloquent ever delivered, and has been translated into almost every language. The tree under which he gave the speech came to be known as Logan's Elm.

The magnificent elm tree, with a span of more than 120 feet and height of 100 feet, fell victim to Dutch Elm disease nearly two centuries later in 1964, but the spot continues to be a state memorial commemorating not only Logan, but other Indian leaders as well. The chief's moving speech has been engraved in marble at the site, and you can also observe a touching footnote placed at the base of a marker by schoolchildren in 1980, closing this sad chapter more than 200 years later.

Logan's Lament

"I appeal to any white man to say, if ever he entered Logan's cabin hungry and I gave him not meat; if ever he came cold or naked and I gave him not clothing. During the course of the last long and bloody war, Logan remained in his tent an advocate for peace. Nay, such was my love for the whites, that those of my own country pointed at me as they passed by and said, 'Logan is the friend of white men.' I had even thought to live with you, but for the injuries of one man. Colonel Cresap, the last spring, in cold blood and unprovoked, cut off all the relatives of Logan; not sparing even my women and children. There runs not a drop of my blood in the veins of any human creature. This called on me for revenge. I have sought it. I have killed many. I have fully glutted my vengeance. For my country, I rejoice at the beams of peace. Yet, do not harbor the thought that mine is the joy of fear. Logan never felt fear. He will not turn on his heel to save his life. Who is there to mourn for Logan? Not one."

POINTS OF INTEREST:

1. *A. W. Marion State Park*
   This park has a 160 acre lake, hiking trails, picnicking, and camping.

2. *Logan Elm Historical Site*
   The memorial is operated by the Ohio Historical Society, and is open daily.

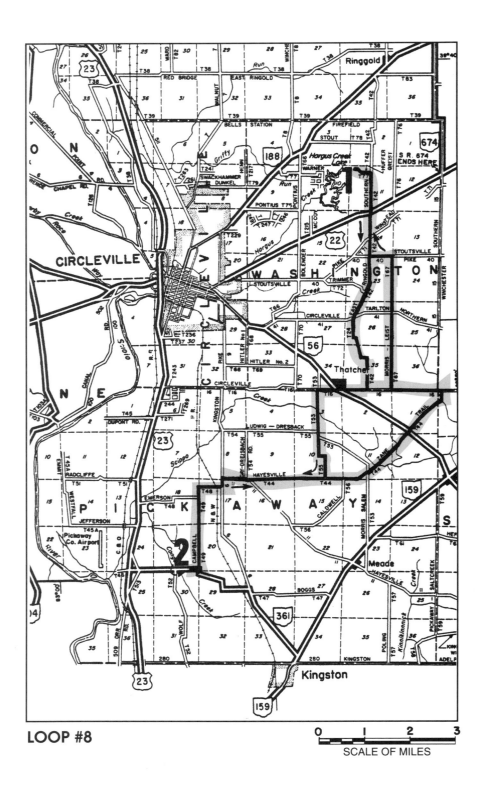

LOOP #8

LOOP #9

Length: 34 miles

Terrain: First half rather hilly, second half flatter

County: Fairfield

The Glacier's Edge

This tour from Lithopolis takes you over rolling hills and through broad valleys, past a covered bridge, a nature preserve, and an unusual old cemetery. It is, indeed, a very beautiful loop, and owes part of its beauty to the master sculptor of thousands of years ago, the glacier. You are entering the edge of the foothills of the Appalachian Plateau, and are crossing terrain where the glacier made its furthest advance before stopping just beyond the southern edge of this loop. The 1,000 foot high ice sheet left behind deposits that covered over the previously eroded landscape, filling and broadening valleys, smoothing hilltops, reversing streams, and creating a more rolling topography than the hilly terrain just to the south. In addition to the glacier's broad strokes, its fine-brush artistry can also be seen on this loop. Looking north from the covered bridge at Rock Mill, you will see a narrow gorge carved in the resistant blackhand sandstone by a tremendous volume of water rushing through here from a draining glacial lake 17,000 years ago. Below the bridge is a huge pothole that was created by the swirling motion of the water carrying sand and pebbles, which scoured into the less resistant sandstone there. The old covered bridge spanning the gorge makes this one of the most picturesque spots anywhere.

Another interesting feature found on this ride is President's (Stonewall) Cemetery, which has been called "America's strangest landmark". This beautifully walled family plot was deeded in 1817 to "James Monroe, President of the United States, and his successors in office forever", in the futile hope of keeping it from being desecrated or plowed over. While a dozen or so early gravestones, many of them broken, can be viewed through the iron gate, no presidents have yet elected to spend eternity here.

33

POINTS OF INTEREST:

1. **Wagnall's Memorial**
   Three public libraries and a community center are housed in this ornate Tudor/Gothic stone building at 150 E. Columbus Street. Open daily.

2. **Rock Mill Covered Bridge and Mill**
   The old mill, built in 1824, has been used as a barn since 1906, and is on private property. The covered bridge, spanning the headwaters of the Hocking River, was built in 1849.

3. **Shallenberger State Nature Preserve**
   Hiking trails are maintained in this beautiful preserve, with one leading up to a look-out that provides a magnificent view of the rolling countryside. There are no facilities here.

4. **President's (Stonewall) Cemetery**

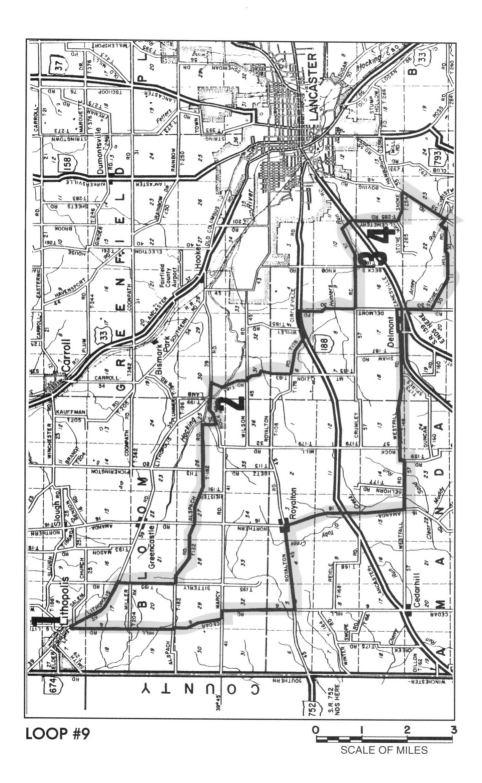

LOOP #9

SCALE OF MILES

0   1   2   3

LOOP #10

Length: 20 miles

Terrain: Hilly

County: Licking

Flint Ridge Tour

This tour can begin at either Flint Ridge Memorial or Black Hand Gorge Nature Preserve. The roads connecting these two beautiful historic sites are hilly, and one section is hard packed dirt with some gravel. The views this loop affords are quite beautiful, and worth the effort to the adventurous traveler. You can start the tour at one site and tour to the other for a picnic, as tables are provided at both.

Flint has played a major role in both the natural history of the land now called Ohio and the history of its people. This loop to Flint Ridge graphically demonstrates the impact of flint. The gemstone was such an important commodity to the early Indians that this area was considered neutral territory and accessible to all. Indians traveled great distances to this five-square mile area to acquire flint, which was used to make tools for fire-making and weapons. Here is found the highest quality flint in the Midwest, and implements made from Flint Ridge flint have been found a thousand miles away.

This layer of hard flint also had another impact on the area. The flint serves as the capstone for this ridge, making it highly resistant to erosion. The surrounding countryside, suffering the effects of erosion, has "fallen" in relation to Flint Ridge, thereby creating the hills you have climbed to reach the memorial. The magnificent views on this tour are, in part, a result of the erosion-resistant flint. Flint has played such a key role that it is now the official gemstone of Ohio.

The nearby Black Hand Gorge bears a historic link to Flint Ridge beyond the fact that they are both now nature preserves. Because of the flint at Flint Ridge, the Licking River became a key transportation link for Indians journeying to Flint Ridge to obtain the stone. You will be retracing that journey, in part, on this tour. The most significant natural feature of Black Hand Gorge is the narrow gorge cut by the Licking River through the blackhand

36

sandstone found here. The name "blackhand" derives from a large dark hand-shaped symbol that once overlooked the gorge from a cliff face. One Indian legend has it that the hand represented sacred Indian territory where no man was to lift his hand against another. The figure was destroyed in 1828 by workmen dynamiting the cliff face to make way for the Ohio-Erie Canal towpath. The remains of the canal locks, and the trolley tunnels that came later, can still be found in the preserve.

To sum up, this loop has nice stops, beautiful scenery, and rough roads—so beware!

POINTS OF INTEREST:

1. *Flint Ridge State Memorial*
   Operated by the Ohio Historical Society, the memorial has hiking trails, a nature preserve, picnic tables, and a museum containing Indian tools and artifacts. An interesting three-dimensional layout of the topography of the area is also on display. The museum is open in the summer Weds.-Sun., weekends in the fall, and closed in the winter. There is an admission charge for the museum.

2. *Route Note:* This road is hard packed dirt with some gravel, and is rough.

3. *Black Hand Gorge State Nature Preserve*
   This preserve is maintained by the Ohio Department of Natural Resources, and is open year round during daylight hours. Picnic tables and hiking trails are provided. *Route Note:* The route through the preserve is a 4.5 mile bike path, and is quite hazardous for cyclists due to joggers, baby carriages, dogs, children, etc. Be careful! (Cars may follow the "north" route on map.)

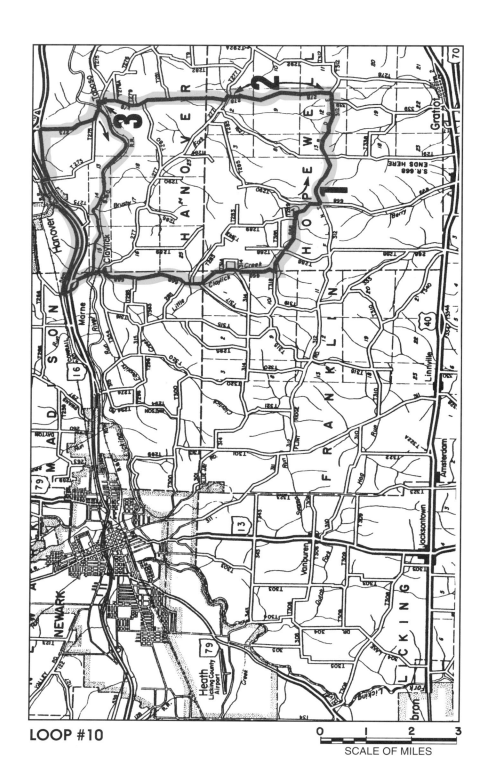

LOOP #10

SCALE OF MILES

0   1   2   3

SECTION II. *Southwest Ohio*

Bear's Mill. Loop #13

Trip Planning Guide
Southwest Ohio

# Name	Length (miles) short loop	Historical site	Nature preserve	Museum	Covered bridge	Pioneer cemetery	Picnic area	Camping (state/county park)	Swimming	Walking trails
*11. The Old Canal Tour	42	X		X	X	X	X	X	X	X
*12. Little Sure-Shot	41		X		X	X	X	X		X
13. The Barn and Field Tour	48 (31)		X			X	X			X
14. The Whispering Oak	58 (30)	X			X	X	X			X
15. Watermills and Waterfalls	19		X				X			X
*16. A 19th Century Sampler	32		X	X	X	X	X	X	X	X
*17. The McGuffey Rider	22	X	X	X			X	X	X	X
18. Germantown	42	X	X		X	X	X			X ·
19. Tecumseh and Friend	27	X	X		X	X	X	X		X
20. 1812 Ohio	34	X	X		X	X	X	X		X
21. Antiques to Antiquity	26	X	X	X	X	X	X			X
22. Ohio's South Sea	45 (32)		X		X	X	X	X	X	X
23. A Lifetime of Change	31 (18)	X			X	X				

* Camp Over Option: <u>Two</u> loops leave from same state park where camping is available

40

Tour Loop Locations
Southwest Ohio

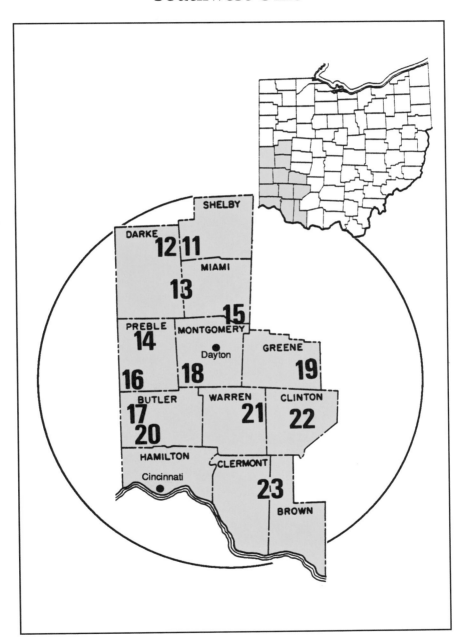

LOOP #11

Length: 42 miles

Terrain: Flat to gently rolling

County: Shelby/Miami

The Old Canal Tour

"There's a little silver ribbon runs across the Buckeye state, Tis the dearest place of all the earth to me."

So begins a song sung by the men who worked more than a century ago during the "balmy days of the old canal". This outing through the gently rolling countryside of Shelby county passes through lush farmland, checkered with corn and wheat fields, and leads the traveler back one-hundred fifty years to the era of the Miami and Erie Canal. Along the way are the traces of Ohio's canal days: canal towns that sprang up along the waterway; the locks that lifted the boats higher and higher on their journey from the Ohio River, over the "Loramie Summit", and on to Lake Erie; the man-made lakes that fed the canal system; and the mills that used her water for power and transport.

In the early years of the nineteenth century, the farmers and merchants of western Ohio did not have ready access to the markets of the rest of the country. They sorely needed a system of roads to transport themselves and their goods to either Lake Erie or the Ohio River, and many points in-between. And so, in 1825, one of the state's first comprehensive highway systems was begun. But this was not a system of pavement; it was a system of water, 249 miles long, comprised of 3 reservoirs, 103 locks, and 19 aqueducts. Because Ohio's streams often flooded in the spring and dried up in the summer, the canal did not use existing natural waterways, but rather carried its own gentle water along manmade channels, in places sharing a valley with a stream or river. Called the "Big Ditch", the canal was completed in 1848, and at its peak nearly 400 boats plied her waters. The power for the canal boats was supplied by mules that walked along the towpath on a 90 foot lead, pulling the boat along at four miles per hour. The mules worked a six hour shift, and the men worked twelve. Each boat had a 2-3 man crew, with a thirteen or fourteen year old boy, called a "hoagie", leading the mules.

Today, as you stop along these last remnants of the old canal, and listen very carefully, perhaps you can still hear the echoes of the young boys driving their mules along the towpath; hear the boatmen calling out to lift the·ropes as their vessels passed in the night by lantern light; feel the bustle of activity at the locks as the water rose and fell with the opening and closing of the gates. And if you listen even more carefully, you might hear in the distance a sound that spelled the beginning of the end of the canal—the shrill whistle of the locomotive as it supplants the "Big Ditch" with its iron tracks. The actual end of the canal in these parts came in 1913, as, perhaps appropriately enough, the Great Miami River rushed out of its banks in that year of the great flood, destroying the canal that shared her valley, returning water to water, and dust to dust.

This loop and the Little Sure-Shot tour both begin at Lake Loramie, providing the option of two days of exploring for campers and other park visitors.

POINTS OF INTEREST:

1. **Lake Loramie State Park**
   The centerpiece of this beautiful state park is Lake Loramie, a manmade reservoir built to furnish water for the canal system. The park has a swimming beach, picnic areas, walking trails, and camping (showers, flush toilets, some electric).

2. **Fort Loramie, Ohio**
   This former trading post, supply fort, and canal town still proudly boasts of its history. Originally established in the mid-1700's as a trading post by the French trader Peter Loramie, and destroyed in 1782 by George Rogers Clark, it was later a supply fort constructed by General "Mad" Anthony Wayne in 1795. A small park is now situated on the old canal right-of-way in the middle of town, where you can see a reconstructed log cabin, read various historical markers, and examine an old canal milestone. The town's museum is located by the park, open limited hours.

3. **Pioneer Cemetery**
   This early cemetery has markers dating back to at least 1822, and the stones of Civil War veterans can be found here. One marker proclaims that the stone was bought by the woman's son "and paid for by him after his sister squandered all her mother's money".

4. **Harmar's Trail Historical Marker**

This marker commemorates General Harmar's Military Trail passing through here in 1790, on his way to a devastating defeat at the hands of the Indians. So poorly conceived and executed were his battle plans that following his defeat, he resigned his commission and returned to Philadelphia, leaving the frontier to men who hoped they would never see him again.

5. **1898 Metal Truss Bridge over Loramie Creek**

A stop here may be rewarded by a glimpse of a great blue heron flying along the stream.

6. **Pickawillany Historical Marker**

This marker commemorates the first English settlement in the West, a trading post built on this site in 1748. Pickawillany was also the site of a thriving Indian Village numbering 4,000 strong at its peak. Occupied by members of several tribes, the Pickawillany Indians referred to themselves as Twigtwees, after the sounds of cranes that lived along the nearby Great Miami River. The village was destroyed by the French in 1752. The marker is located on Hardin Road about 100 yards south of Hardin Road Alt.

7. **Piqua Historical Area**

Operated by the Ohio Historical Society, you can take an actual "mule-powered" canal boat ride here on a restored section of the Miami-Erie Canal. An Indian museum and prehistoric earthwork are also found here, and tours of the farm of Indian agent John Johnston, restored to 1829, are available. The site is open Weds.-Sun., in the summer, and weekends in Sept. and Oct. Admission charge.

8. **Loramie Mill**

Built in 1851, this mill is no longer in service. Located on private property, it can be clearly seen from the road. Across the road from the mill is a set of canal locks, also on private property. The mill can be seen by turning right from Hardin Road onto Landman Mill Road. After you pass the mill, turn left at the end of the steel bridge. then left on Piqua-Lockington Road.

9. *Lockington Locks*

Another Ohio Historical Society site, a series of five original stone locks is located here. You can walk along the locks and read the informative markers explaining their operation. To reach the locks, turn left on Fessler-Buxton Road (Museum Trail). There is no charge.

10. *Lockington Reserve*

Picnic tables, latrines, and hiking trails are found here at the reserve, where the Lockington Dam is located.

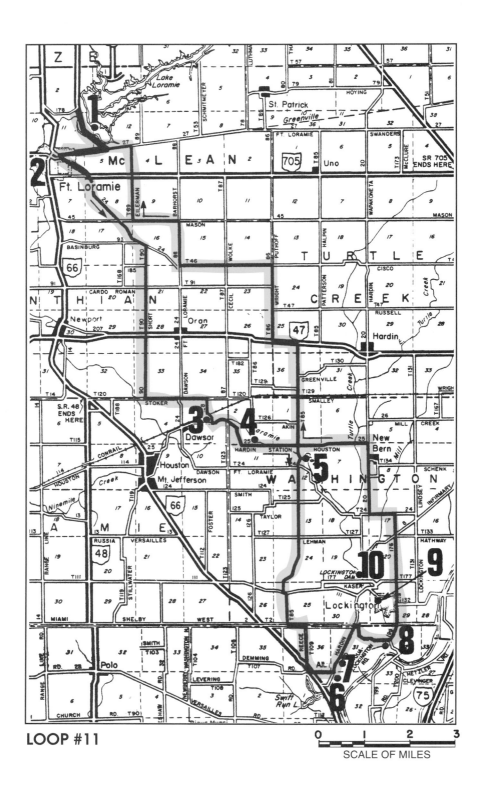

LOOP #11

SCALE OF MILES

0   1   2   3

LOOP #12

Length: 41 miles

Terrain: Flat

County: Shelby/Darke

Little Sure-Shot

This ramble through the rural countryside of western Ohio takes the traveler through the crossroads community where one of America's most famous women was born, past the fields that played such an important part in her childhood, and finally to the little cemetery in Darke County where she now rests. Along the way, you'll pass beneath the towering spires of several country churches that are on the National Register of Historic Places, ride along the shore of scenic Lake Loramie, and visit one of Ohio's earliest communities. You'll travel ridgetops just high enough to provide sweeping views of the checkered countryside that stretches to the horizon, the fields especially striking in late summer when they blaze a brilliant gold and rust.

Phoebe Ann Moses was born in a log cabin at Willodell, Ohio on August 13, 1860. Her father died when she was quite young, and soon these fields echoed with the crack of her rifle as she hunted game for her family. Her skill was especially appreciated by the illustrious guests at the Golden Lamb in Lebanon, where they dined on her quarry—and never found any buckshot in their meals. When Annie, as her sisters called her, was fifteen years old, she was "put up" to a shooting match with the champion marksman and performer Frank Butler. The contest took place near Cincinnati at a place called Oakley, and when this teenaged girl won the match, the legend of Annie Oakley was born.

Annie and Frank Butler married a year later and began touring, putting on shooting exhibitions that eventually led to her starring in Buffalo Bill's Wild West Show. She performed all over the world, and her command performance at Queen Victoria's Jubilee had more royalty assembled for an outdoor show than any before. She was even reported to have shot a cigarette from the mouth of Kaiser Wilhelm. In 1883, she was introduced to Sitting Bull, who was convinced that, because of her great skill, she was

47

possessed of, and protected by, the Great Spirit. He adopted her, and named her "Watanya Cicilia", or Little Sure-Shot.

Annie maintained her skill and continued to tour throughout most of her years, but it was to these gently rolling fields of Darke County that she returned at the end of her life. She died on November 3, 1926, and eighteen days later, Frank Butler, her husband of fifty years, also passed away. The Greenville Daily Advocate reported in its full front-page story, "here, among the people of her native heath, she will ever be remembered for her winsomeness, her sincerity, and her love of the country in which she was born, and in whose broad expanse she chose to have her ashes laid. In the years to come, her grave will be a shrine for those who loved this woman, before whom the kings and rulers of the world bowed and paid tribute, and whom all honored."

Although less famous than Annie Oakley, another man's monuments stand majestically above the fields as you head back toward Lake Loramie. Anton Goehr's work was for the glory of God, and this master carpenter helped construct some twenty churches in the area. The stunning twin spires that stand sentinel over the community of Minster were his handiwork in 1872, and the magnificent church in Fort Loramie was crafted by him in 1881. He so loved his work that he requested his grave marker be made of wood, and upon his death in 1885, his wish was granted. His wooden marker stands in St. Augustine Cemetery, and a plaque on the rear of the marker lists the names of the people who keep his marker painted each year.

This loop and The Old Canal Tour both originate at Lake Loramie, providing the option of two days of exploring for park visitors and campers.

POINTS OF INTEREST:

1. **Lake Loramie State Park**
   The tour begins at this state park, which features beautiful Lake Loramie. A swimming beach, picnic areas, and camping with showers, flush toilets, and some electric sites are available.

2. **Fort Loramie, Ohio**
   As you enter this historic town you'll pass by St. Michael's Church, built in 1881. This old canal town also has a park with historical markers, and a small museum is open limited hours.

3. **St. Paul's Lutheran Cemetery**
You may want to brush up on your German if you stop here, as many of the early markers are inscribed in that language.

4. **Willodell, Ohio**
Annie Oakley was born in a log cabin near this little crossroads community.

5. **Speelman Cemetery**
At the back of this little roadside cemetery lies Erasmus Paulsel, a confederate soldier buried in the North under a military marker of the Confederate States of America. A Union soldier is buried at the other end of the cemetery.

6. **Frenchtown, Ohio**
As you pass through this early community of French settlers, you'll see the Sainte Famille Church, built in 1866 and now on the National Register.

7. **Brock Cemetery**
Here lies Annie Oakley and husband Frank Butler, along with her brother and his wife and children.

8. **1850 Log House**
This dilapidated structure was an early log house, and the logs are visible where the siding has fallen off. It is private property.

9. **Indian Trail Road**
This short stretch of road follows the Greenville Treaty Line of 1795. Land to the north was Indian Territory, and land to the south was opened for settlement.

10. **St. Augustine Cemetery**
The small chapel at the west end of the cemetery was built in 1855 by Mr. Steinemann as a memorial in Thanksgiving after his wife recovered from a serious illness. Anton Goehr, church builder and woodcarver, is buried near the chapel.

11. **Minster, Ohio**
A side trip through the streets of this charming town is a delight. Be sure to stop by St. Augustine Church with its twin spires and eight clock faces. The church is on the National Register.

LOOP #12

0   1   2   3

SCALE OF MILES

LOOP #13

Length: 48 miles
(31 miles on short loop)

Terrain: Mostly flat, some hills by river

County: Miami/Darke

The Barn and Field Tour

The backroad buff's answer to the city's House and Garden Tour, this Barn and Field Tour begins at a prairie nature preserve, winds along country lanes, traverses wide open countryside, and finally meanders along the banks of the scenic Stillwater River. Along the way, you'll cross old steel bridges above cascading streams, pass by neatly manicured fields bordered by beautiful stone fences; and see several unusual octagonal barns and a unique round barn. Pioneer cemeteries, a working water-powered mill, and a scattering of old log structures round out the loop.

There are few scenes more enchanting than that of a freshly painted red barn standing watch over a field of golden wheat under an azure sky, with a whirring, spinning windmill casting its hypnotic spell. Long ignored by the serious school of architecture, the American barn is now finally receiving its due, just as it approaches endangerment as a species. As the old wooden covered bridge is being replaced by concrete decks and railings, so is the big red barn being replaced by the sterile and unimaginative metal pole building. The function of the old barn can be replaced, but its magic and charm, built into its hand-hewn timbers and beams, is irreplaceable.

Perhaps the most functional, and one of the most beautiful barns, is the bank barn, several of which can be seen on this tour. The bank barn was originally designed to be built into a hillside, allowing the wagons to be driven into the second or "upper" floor from the hillside, and allowing the animals to walk into the "lower" floor on the other side. So popular was the design that it was adopted even in the flat land of western Ohio, with dirt banks leading up to the main doors in place of the hillside. These barns usually face south to allow for the warming rays of the winter sun to shine into the animals' quarters, while the "bank" on the north side serves to block the cold north wind.

Another feature of the early barn is the high roof over the mow, permitting the storage of loose hay, but modern field balers have eliminated the need for such high roofs.

While bank barns and "plain" barns are quite common, another type of barn is very rare: the octagonal barn. Only about a dozen of these multi-faceted diamonds exist in all of southwest Ohio. The four octagonal barns on this loop were all built in the 1890's, and were additions to rectangular barns of the 1870's. Were they a short lived fad, or did they serve some special purpose? All of these unusual barns remain in use, and while clearly in view from the road, are, of course, on private property.

No barn tour would be complete without the most rare and unusual barn of all: the truly round barn. A cone-shaped roof protruding from a cornfield signals your approach to the only round barn in Darke County, and one of the very few in all of Ohio. Like the octagonals, this round red barn, built around 1900, is situated right along the road, although on private property.

With its wonderful collection of octagonal, round, and bank barns, this area would be a leading contender for a "historic barn district", honoring the fortitude and ingenuity of the farmers who designed and constructed them a century ago.

POINTS OF INTEREST:

1. **Stillwater Prairie Reserve**
   This beautiful 217 acre nature preserve, operated by the Miami County Park District, is open daily during daylight hours. The preserve features a boardwalk, two ponds, a path along the scenic Stillwater River, and, of course, a prairie, where one may find unusual and beautiful prairie plants and flowers. One portion of the prairie can only be reached by wading the shallow Stillwater River, quite a treat on a hot day! Picnic areas are also located here, making this a truly nice place to begin and end this loop.

2. **One-Room Schoolhouse**
   This abandoned, deteriorating schoolhouse was probably built in the late 1800's.

3. **Octagonal Barn**

4. **Octagonal Barn**

5. *St. Peter's Evangelical Lutheran Log Church*
   Although now covered with wood siding, this charming little church is actually constructed of logs. Built in 1850, it may well be the only surviving log church from the settlement days of western Ohio. The little church has not seen regular worship since 1905. The adjoining cemetery has, among its several markers, a rusty gate standing in the line of tombstones, dated 1865.

6. *Webster, Ohio*
   This small community sits on a millrace across from the Stillwater River, and still boasts several of its early brick homes. You will note an unusually small barn, complete with cupola nearly the size of the roof, as you pass through this tiny community.

7. *1889 Barn*
   The unusual roof of this large barn gives it quite a striking appearance. A good example of a bank barn sits in a rolling pasture just south of this barn. Both barns are on private property.

8. *Erisman Pioneer Cemetery*

9. *Round Barn*
   Built around 1900, this is the only round barn in Darke County, and one of the very few in all of Ohio.

10. *Martin Pioneer Cemetery*
    George Fifer Adams, a soldier of the Revolutionary War, is buried in this old cemetery, as are veterans of the War of 1812 and Civil War.

11. *Bear's Mill*
    Built in 1849 by Gabriel Baer, this mill is in operation today, milling flour and meal with burr stones, powered by water flowing through a millrace beneath the mill. You may tour this vast structure and see the huge hand-hewn timbers inside. The mill is open Thurs.-Fri. 11-5, Sat. 9-5 and Sun. 11-5.

12. *Octagonal Barn*

13. *Octagonal Barn*

14. *The Scenic Stillwater*
    The old brick Stillwater Church and adjoining cemetery, nestled by an old metal bridge, signals the beginning of a scenic stretch along the Stillwater River. Many of the nearby buildings and fences are constructed of the native stone from the valley.

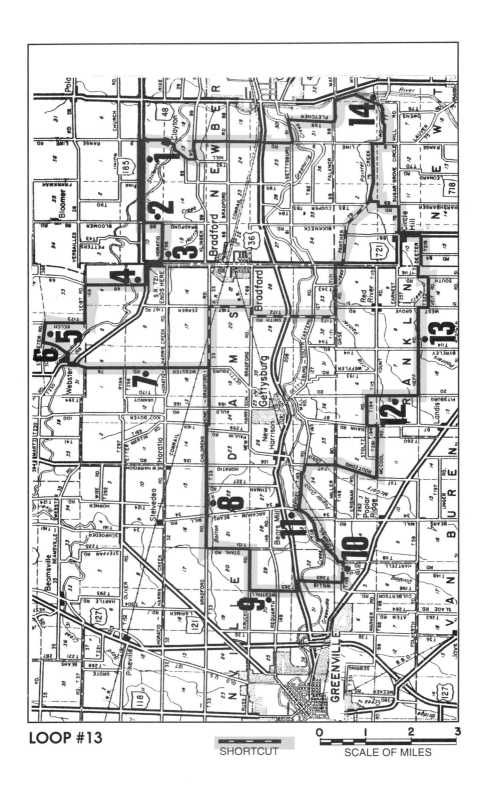

LOOP #13

SHORTCUT

SCALE OF MILES

0 1 2 3

LOOP #14

Length: 58 miles
(30 miles on short loop)

Terrain: Flat to gently rolling

County: Preble/Darke

The Whispering Oak

On a windy morning in Preble County, Ohio, on the outskirts of Eaton, if the breezes are just right and you listen very carefully, you can hear the tale of the titanic struggle that took place here nearly two centuries ago. So intense was the struggle between the American forces and the Indian warriors that it echoes through time to this day, told and retold by a witness who was there to see it—the majestic Whispering Oak. The names of those who gave their lives in the struggle are on the wind that rustles through the legendary tree—Williams, Jett, Clinton, Bowling, English, Hale; the names of the generals who led their troops to disastrous defeats—Harmar and St. Clair; the names of the great Indian chiefs who led their warriors to victory—Blue Jacket, Little Turtle, Black Hoof, Tarhe; the name of a young Indian scout— Tecumseh; and the name of the conquering "American general who never slept"—Anthony Wayne.

The years 1790-1795 were the most critical in the future state of Ohio's history, and the ground that the traveler covers on this loop was perhaps the most struggled for. The Indians had been giving way steadily as the settlers came over the mountains and down the Ohio River, establishing settlements mostly along the Kentucky side. The great chiefs saw the need to draw the line on white encroachment at the Ohio River, and this set the stage for the Indian Wars throughout western Ohio.

After more than 1,500 settlers had been attacked along the Ohio River, President George Washington sent Gen. Josiah Harmar to crush the Indians and open the Ohio Country to settlement. However, marching from Fort Washington in Cincinnati, it was Harmar who was crushed. Fear increased along the frontier, and Washington sent Gen. Arthur St. Clair to march out of Fort Washington. St. Clair's march was somewhat more successful— he managed to build Fort Hamilton and Fort Jefferson before being thoroughly routed and defeated. Near panic swept the frontier.

The next general sent was "Mad" Anthony Wayne. As preparations were made for this third campaign, Col. Wilkinson constructed Fort St. Clair to fill the gap between Fort Hamilton (Hamilton, Ohio) and Fort Jefferson, as he deemed it too far between forts. This string of forts ultimately reached into northwest Ohio to the Maumee River, and proved decisive. The Battle of Fallen Timbers meant victory for the American army, but the land watched over by the Whispering Oak saw more Indian victories than American. A weather-beaten, nearly illegible marker on top of a mound in a nearby cemetery records in stone what the wind whispers: "In memory of Lt. John Lowery of the 2nd sub-legion - Ensign Boyd of the 1st and thirteen non-commissioned officers and privates who fell about five miles north of this place in an obstinate engagement with the Indians on the 17th day of October, 1793. Lt. Lowery was from New Jersey and had served with reputation in the levies of 1791 under General St. Clair. Ensign Boyd was a young man of much promise; they were in command of an escort of ninety men having charge of twenty wagons loaded with provisions and stores for the Army of Gen. Wayne."

As you travel from the historical site of Fort St. Clair to the site of Fort Jefferson, you'll pass by pioneer cemeteries, an old stone water tower, beautiful century-old country churches, a covered bridge, charming farmhouses, abandoned schoolhouses, and more. All seems peaceful and serene as you travel along the route but be sure to listen to the wind.

POINTS OF INTEREST:

1. *Fort St. Clair*
   Owned by the Ohio Historical Society, this was the site of Fort St. Clair, built in 1792. Although the fort itself is long gone, the area has picnic tables, hiking trails, and shelter houses. It is open daily April-October. Here is found the Whispering Oak, and beneath it the graves of six soldiers who were ambushed on Nov. 6, 1792.

2. **Mound Hill Union Cemetery**

    Section 7 of this historic cemetery includes an Indian mound topped by a monument to fifteen American soldiers killed by Indians in 1793. Veterans of the Revolutionary War and the Battle of Gettysburg are buried in nearby sections, and a marker shaped like a mill marks the resting place of the town's early miller. Enter the cemetery at its first entrance on Rt. 122. After your stop here, continue east on Rt. 122, then make a sharp left onto Seven Mile Drive just past the bridge. Follow this road out of town.

3. **Stone Water Tower**

    Located in Eaton's Water Works Park, you'll ride past this beautiful old tower on your way out of town. It has been out of use for many years, and is dwarfed by its successor rising up beside it.

4. **Christman Covered Bridge**

    This charming bridge was built in 1895 at the time when debate raged over wooden versus iron bridges. Built by Everett Sherman at a cost of $2,452, the bridge solved the travelers' problem of having to ford Seven Mile Creek at this point.

5. **One-Room Schoolhouse**

    The privies and water pump still stand at this old abandoned schoolhouse, although no longer in use.

6. **Stump Pioneer Cemetery**

7. **1881 United Brethren Church**

8. **Mills Pioneer Cemetery**

    This small cemetery makes an interesting stop, as you'll find handcarved markers of broken slate, a marker to a veteran of the Spanish-American War, and a large monument to Lydia Mills Hutton, dated 1887, which humbly proclaims that she "lived a life as pure as that of the Virgin Mary".

9. **Fort Jefferson**

    Operated by the Ohio Historical Society, this is the site of Fort Jefferson, built by St. Clair in 1791 and later used as a supply fort by Anthony Wayne. The site has water, picnic tables, and a shelterhouse. Markers denoting several aspects of the now vanished fort help the visitor mentally reconstruct the scene.

10. U.M. Church and Pioneer Cemetery
While resting at Fort Jefferson, you may wish to visit the lovely old church across the street. The early cemetery adjoining the church is the final resting place of veterans of the Revolutionary War, War of 1812, and the Mexican War.

11. Ithaca, Ohio
This little village still has many of its early brick buildings.

12. Log Home
This example of an early log home stands in a meadow on private property just west of the main loop.

13. Geeting Covered Bridge
In 1894, this picturesque bridge replaced the foot log that spanned Price Creek. Dave Geeting, the neighboring farmer, was excited to be the first person to drive his horse and buggy through the bridge. It had its roof blown off in a storm in 1914, but was repaired.

14. Route Note
Be cautious on Eaton-Lewisburg Road, as it can be rather busy, especially in late afternoon. As you enter Eaton, go south on Rt. 127 from Eaton-Lewisburg Rd., then right on Debbie Drive. You can now retrace your route back to Fort St. Clair.

15. Roberts Covered Bridge Side Trip
To visit the relocated and restored bridge in Eaton, continue south on S.R. 127 (Barron St.) through town to St. Clair (R), then to Beech St. (R). This rare double-barrelled covered bridge, one of the oldest in the nation, was built in 1829, and restored in 1991.

Short loop: If you, like Colonel Wilkinson, feel the distance is too long between forts on this ride, a short-cut is shown on the map by a dashed line. This alternative loop is about 30 miles in length.

Christman Covered Bridge, Preble County

Geeting Covered Bridge, Preble County

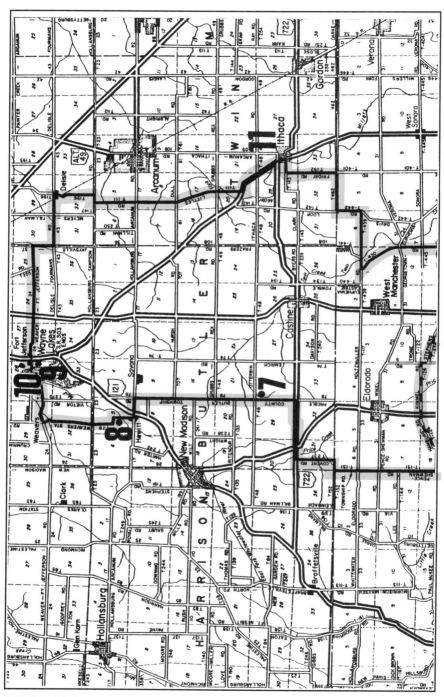

LOOP #14
Northern Half

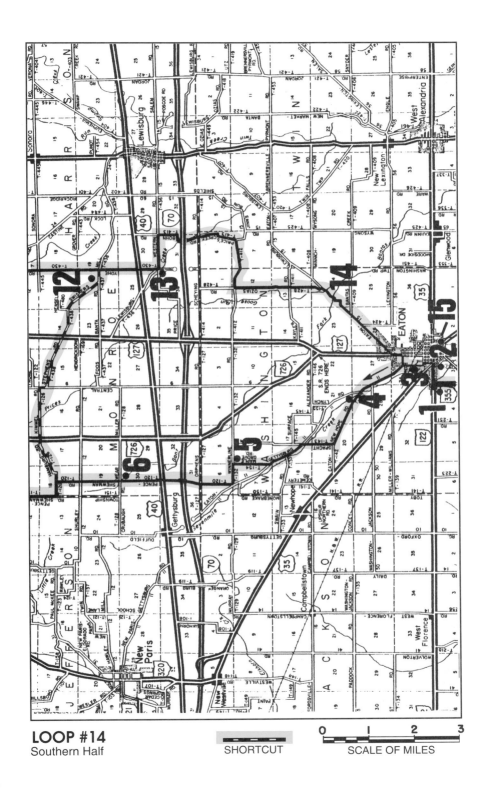

LOOP #14
Southern Half

SHORTCUT

0   1   2   3

SCALE OF MILES

LOOP #15

Length: 19 miles

Terrain: Rolling

County: Miami/Montgomery

Watermills and Waterfalls

This 19 mile loop takes the traveler from the outer residential fringes of northern Montgomery County into the rolling country-side of Miami County, passing by old canal locks and through an 1841 restoration of Tippecanoe City, across iron bridges and along a winding lane that meanders by the oldest gristmill still standing in Ohio, and returns to a nature preserve featuring tumbling water falls and gurgling streams. The tour's proximity to Dayton makes it a convenient tonic for persons seeking an escape from the bustle of the city.

There are few symbols of our Ohio heritage more romantic than the old mill. Songwriters, poets, and painters have all extolled the virtues of the gristmill of days gone by, making the mill a symbol of simpler, more tranquil times. The farmer of yester-year would sack up his "grist" of corn or wheat, toss it across the back of his horse, and then, straddling the load, head to the mill to wait his turn having it ground into meal or flour. The early mills used burrs for grinding, crushing the corn or wheat between two huge circular millstones. The flour, bran, and "middlings" were then sacked up in the same bag, being tied off into sections by string, and placed across the horse's back for the return trip home. This was, of course, the part of the trip the horse preferred, as the miller kept one-eighth of the grain as payment. The grumbling of the farmer that the bag was even lighter than that fell on unsympathetic ears as man and beast made their way slowly down the road.

The ravages of time and progress have reduced the number of mills still standing in Ohio to a relative few, their only trace often being a stone foundation by a waterway. It is a rare treat when one can see an early wooden gristmill, albeit no longer in service, standing along the lane, in such good condition that it looks much the same as it must have one-hundred seventy years ago, in a setting that time has forgotten, creating a living portrait of the nineteenth century.

While Ohio may have been noted for its early mills, it is less famous for its waterfalls; nevertheless, there are many Ohio cascades that are quite beautiful, including Charleston Falls, where our loop comes full circle. By virtue of overrunning a rock escarpment that is also found in Canada and New York State, this little stream, falling thirty-seven feet to the rocks below, claims a distant kinship with the great Niagara. The sylvan setting, the horseshoe-shaped falls, and the shaded valley below create a picture of beauty, while the tumbling water draws a curtain of sound around this natural jewel, making it a perfect place for quiet reflection.

POINTS OF INTEREST:

1. **Charleston Falls Preserve**
   This beautiful nature preserve is home to waterfalls, streams, ledges, two miles of trails, a pond, prairie, and an observation tower. A picnic area and drinking water are available, but restrooms are not. Operated by the Miami County Park District, the preserve is open during daylight hours.

2. **Old Canal Road**
   Be cautious of workday truck traffic near a quarry on this road that follows the old canal.

3. **Tipp City**
   The traveler will pass through an 1841 restoration area called Tippecanoe City, where an old roller mill and other nineteenth century buildings are found. Old ads preserved on the building sides add a charming touch, and antique buffs will enjoy the several shops located here. A canal lock is preserved beside the roller mill.

4. **The Old Staley Mill**
   This may well be the oldest gristmill still standing in Ohio. Originally built by Mr. Wrench in 1818, it allegedly ground meal for the Indians. Elias Staley bought the mill in 1824, and the mill and road bear his name to this day. The mill stands on private property.

   Route Note
   Due to the loop's proximity to Dayton, the traveler should be prepared for somewhat more vehicular traffic, particularly on the southern portion of this tour.

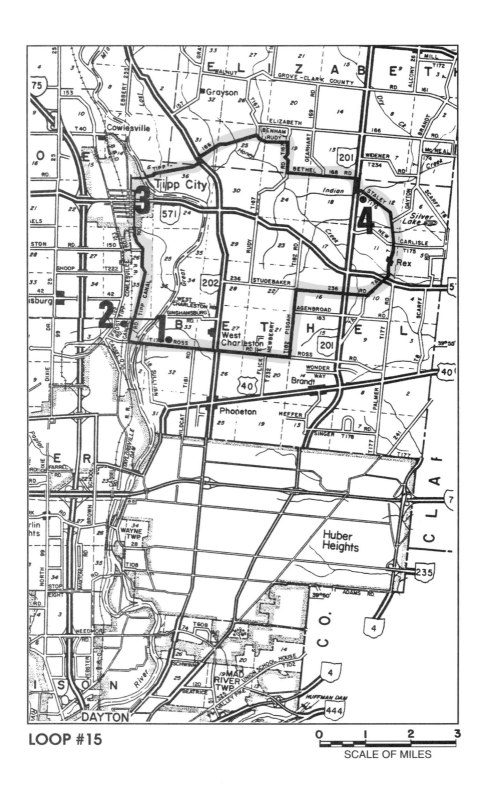

LOOP #15

SCALE OF MILES

0   I   2   3

LOOP #16

Length: 32 miles

Terrain: Rolling

County: Preble

A 19th Century Sampler

This 32 mile tour through the rolling countryside of Preble County, Ohio, near the Indiana border, clearly describes the word "charming". Natural beauty and wildlife abound as you travel through time in an area that has changed little since the 1800's. Magnificent farmhouses, old log homes, historic country churches, abandoned one room schoolhouses, and other sign-posts of the past beckon from a century ago as you sojourn along these quiet country lanes and through sleepy rural ham-lets. Bobwhites call from the fields as red-tailed hawks circle overhead; kingfishers chatter and great blue herons glide along the streams as you ride back in time nearly one-hundred years, to the days of the horse and buggy. It is 1894 in southwest Ohio.

As the whirring of your wheels changes to the clip-clop of hooves while you travel along the road to the country store in Fairhaven, you recall the days when this quiet little town saw some pretty raucous behavior on Saturday nights. The three-story red-brick building that houses the country store (later to become an antique shop) was originally a tavern building, built in 1832 to cater to the drovers who drove their livestock through Fairhaven on the way to the Ohio River. The women from the town came to the Bunker Hill House on Saturday nights to dance with the drovers in the ballroom above the tavern room. The coming of the railroad in 1865 spelled the end of the cattle drives here, the tavern closed, and the building became a country store.

As you continue your ride northward along the Concord-Fairhaven Road, you can hear the sounds of the hammers as they put the finishing touches on the new covered bridge spanning Fourmile Creek. Mr. Sherman has just finished another one, and steps back to read the sign above the portal: "$10 Fine for Riding or Driving Faster than a Walk over this Bridge". You stop to enjoy the view of the stream through the small square window cut in the side of the bridge, placed there both out of considera-

65

tion and to keep folks from making their own "windows". Everett Sherman has been busy since he moved here after the big storm of May 12, 1886 that destroyed many of the county's original twenty-nine covered bridges. He builds them well, and economically, using an expired patent of Horace Childs. This unusual design is found in only one place outside Preble County—and that's the one he built in Delaware County before moving here.

You see a white steeple looming up ahead, so taking your leave of the bridge, you canter toward the church and its welcome water pump in the churchyard. After refreshing yourself, you continue your journey past a one-room schoolhouse where the children are playing in the schoolyard, and then, as you turn south toward Morning Sun, your thoughts turn to the upcoming Sunday service at the Hopewell Church. For many of the earliest pioneer families, the thread that bound them together was the Hopewell Church. Old Hopewell began as a log church, built by Scotch-Irish families who moved to the Ohio wilderness in 1808 from Hopewell, South Carolina because they opposed slavery. In 1825, the members built a new brick church, making and drying the bricks right in the churchyard. Even the floor was brick, with each family paving under its own pew. The area became a stop on the underground railroad, and a bench was provided along one wall of the church, specifically for any Negroes passing through the area who might wish to worship. "Mother Hopewell" gave rise to four daughter-churches between 1834 and 1870, including ones in Fairhaven and Morning Sun, and she herself was refurbished in 1880.

As you come to the end of your ride, you begin to notice that the sound of clip-clopping is changing back to the whir of your wheels. The downhill coast to the park will help you gain enough speed to get through the time warp and back to the present, where a refreshing swim awaits you at the beach at Hueston Woods.

POINTS OF INTEREST:

1. *Hueston Woods State Park*
   The tour begins at Hedgerow Picnic Area in the north end of the park, just east of the campground, off Loop Road. This full-facility park has camping, a lodge, cabins, swimming beach, nature programs, hiking trails, and more.

2. *Bowstring Bridge*
   This very unique metal bowstring bridge was probably built around 1870.

3. **Fairhaven, Ohio**
   This quaint town looks much the same as it must have more than a century ago, for a large number of its original buildings have been maintained or restored. The most dominant building on the street through the town is the Bunker Hill House, on the west side of Route 177. A Hopewell "daughter-church", now the Fairhaven United Presbyterian Church, still stands, and a log building reputed to be the 1808 Hopewell rectory can be seen on the east side of the street. Fairhaven is a popular antique spot on Sundays.

4. **Harshman Covered Bridge**
   Spanning Fourmile Creek in a beautiful pastoral setting, the Harshman Covered Bridge was built in 1894 by Everett Sherman at a cost of $3,184. The "$10.00 Fine" sign is long gone.

5. **1881 Country Church**
   This picturesque church has seen little alteration, and a working hand water pump still stands in the churchyard.

6. **Early Log House**
   Across the street from the church, on private property, stands a small one-room log house. Built prior to 1850, it was moved to this location several years ago.

7. **One-Room Schoolhouse**
   This old abandoned schoolhouse was probably built around 1880.

8. **Morning Sun, Ohio**
   This small hamlet is dominated by the white steeple of the Morning Sun Church, built in 1870. It is another daughter-Hopewell. As you leave Morning Sun, you will pass by an old tractor graveyard and see the former Morning Sun Schoolhouse, built in 1915.

9. **The Hopewell Church**
   This historic church, built in 1825, is open for non-denominational services on summer Sunday mornings. The adjacent cemetery, with its beautiful stone wall, is the township's oldest, and dates back to 1808. Dr. Alexander Porter, the church's first pastor, is buried here.

10. **Route Note**
    Be cautious as you travel the last mile from the church to the park, as the road is quite curvy here. Be sure to stay to the right.

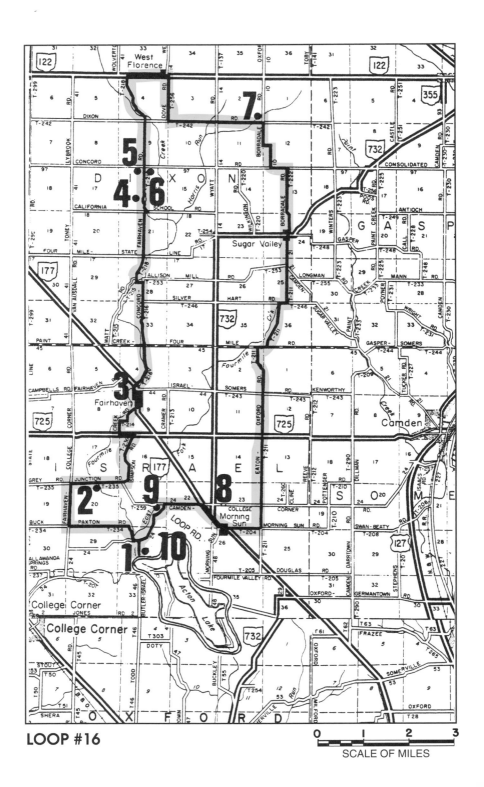

LOOP #16

0   I   2   3

SCALE OF MILES

LOOP #17

Length: 22 miles

Terrain: Rather hilly

County: Butler

The McGuffey Rider

This loop from beautiful Hueston Woods in northwest Butler County takes the traveler through panoramic countryside, past abandoned one-room schoolhouses, back to the early days of readin', 'ritin', and 'rithmetic, to the home of the man who changed education on the frontier and throughout the nation. Along the way, the route winds through a state park, past a magnificent woods, along country lanes, and through the charming town of Oxford, Ohio.

It was in Oxford, one-hundred-fifty years ago, that Miami University professor William Holmes McGuffey penned "A is for Ax" in the first McGuffey Reader, replacing themes of pessimism and death with lessons about the frontier, infused with a spirit necessary to build a new society. McGuffey's Readers became so popular that he soon was known as the "schoolmaster of the nation", and the number of his Readers published is surpassed only by the Holy Bible. Although first published in 1836, the books are still in use in some of America's schools today. The brick house that McGuffey built in Oxford also served as an informal school where he taught the neighborhood children on the front porch as he formulated and developed his new ideas about education.

As you travel the rolling scenic road to Oxford, you will pass by an abandoned one-room schoolhouse built in 1879. Almost certainly this old brick schoolhouse echoed with the voices of young students practicing their "articulation, inflection, accent, and gestures" as they read aloud from their Readers. The old walls of the schoolhouse have heard countless recitations of Longfellow, Emerson, Whittier, and scores of other great writers found in McGuffey's books.

Although A stood for ax for the generation of Ohio's students a century and a half ago, the ax spelled annihilation for the state's magnificent forest. For centuries upon centuries, Ohio was

69

covered by perhaps the greatest forest in the world, with trees towering more than fifty feet to the first limb. The forest was so extensive that the settlers breathed a sigh of relief upon reaching one of the few breaks in the forest canopy, where perhaps a small prairie thrived. But in only a blink of Mother Nature's eye, the pioneers cleared the land, converting the forest into fields, log houses, barns, and ash heaps.

Although the forest was virtually eradicated from Ohio, a few vestigial plots survived. Mathew Hueston, a soldier under "Mad" Anthony Wayne, returned to this area after his service in 1797 and acquired several thousand acres of land. Two-hundred acres were left uncut, and have survived through the centuries. Today, this magnificent woodland serves as a window in time through which we can look back and see the forest primeval before the arrival of the settlers. As one walks the trails beneath these mighty trees in Hueston Woods State Nature Preserve, one cannot escape feeling the majesty of this natural cathedral. A also stands for Awe.

"The 19th Century Sampler" tour also begins at Hueston Woods, providing another day ride for campers and other park visitors.

POINTS OF INTEREST:

1. *Hueston Woods State Park*
   This full-facility park offers camping, a lodge, cabins, swimming beach, hiking trails, nature programs, and more. The tour begins at the Hedgerow Picnic area at the north end of the park, just east of the campground, off Loop Road.

2. *Hueston Woods State Nature Preserve*
   This National Natural Landmark is located within the boundaries of the park, near your turn onto Brown Road from Loop Road.

3. *Pioneer Farm and House Museum*
   Built in 1832, this pioneer house is open summer weekends 12-4, and is also within Hueston Woods State Park.

4. *One-Room Schoolhouse*
   This abandoned schoolhouse was built in 1879, and is typical of the one-room schoolhouses of the day.

5. *McGuffey Museum*

Located in Oxford at Spring and Oak Streets, this house that McGuffey built is now a National Landmark. McGuffey's unique eight-sided desk can be seen at a west window. The museum is open 2-4 on weekends, closed August.

6. *City Park Picnic Area*

7. *Route Note*

The paved surface becomes a little rough on the return portion of the loop, slowing you just enough to allow for your full enjoyment of the panorama of farms and fields, woods and streams, as you tour these rural ridgetops.

CONSIDER THE TREE

Consider the tree,
whose fitting task it is
to inter-knit the earth and sky
in one well drawn togetherness
of soil and sun,
as, from the deepest root,
a bit of earth is taken,
transformed, transported far
into the topmost tendril tip
to texture there
a new born leaf
joining into sky;
a motion matched,
in fitting need,
as, from the highest leaf,
a bit of sun-lit air is taken,
transformed, transported far
into the deepest fibril tip
to texture there
a newborn root,
joining into earth
to make the living tree
symbol of
THE FITTING ONE
that, inter-living earth and sky,
gives birth to wholeness on the way
and gives to me
a birthplace, too,
for emerging life in me,
as I stand among the trees
and let them knit
a universe
on a Sunday afternoon.

Ross L. Mooney

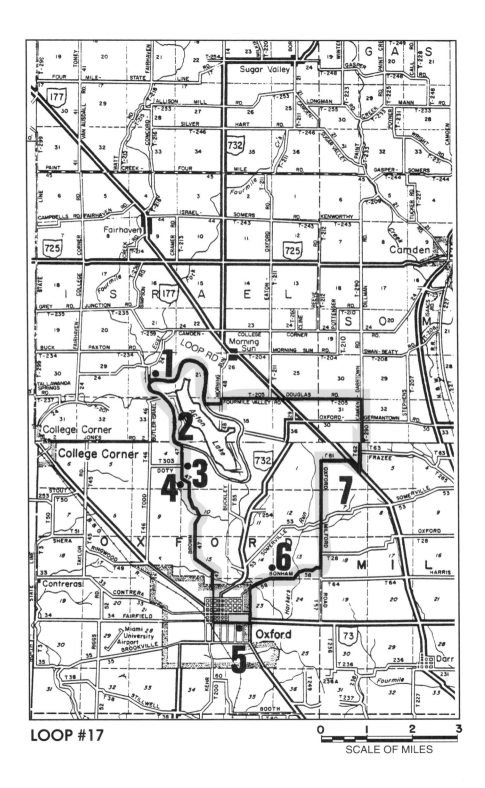

LOOP #17

SCALE OF MILES

0 1 2 3

LOOP #18

Length: 42 miles

Terrain: Flat to rolling, with a few steep hills

County: Montgomery/Preble

Germantown

This rolling tour from southwestern Montgomery County into Preble County is delightful for the scenery alone, but add the covered bridges, old mills and churches, historic inns and homes to the vistas of the twin valleys and their riffled streams, and a truly pleasurable outing is at hand. The terrain is as diverse as the points of interest, ranging from flat to rolling, with a few steep hills along the way.

As you begin your tour from the Germantown Reserve, you can see the route winding ahead through the valley below, leading to the charming village of Germantown and back one-hundred years in time to its historic downtown area, which is listed on the National Register. The centerpiece of Germantown is the Florentine Hotel, built in 1816-17, making it the second oldest inn in Ohio. As you pass beneath its wrought iron balcony, you can picture such notables as Henry Clay exhorting the crowds gathered in the street below. A ride through the side streets of the town reveals several more early and well-preserved structures, and the ads on the alley-sides of the buildings, including an old "Bull Durham" sign, are interesting as well. To leave Germantown, head north on Cherry Street, which becomes Diamond Mill Road.

While the brick homes of Germantown are from the mid-nineteenth century, an example of an even earlier home can be found on the grounds of the Preble County Historical Society at Swartsel Farm. This restored log home dates back to 1813, when it was built in nearby Lewisburg, Ohio. The keen eyed observer will spot at least one other old log home along the loop that is still in service as a residence.

POINTS OF INTEREST:

1. **Germantown Reserve**
   Operated by the Dayton-Montgomery County Park District, the Re-

74

serve has hiking trails through mature forest, picnicking near scenic overlooks, and restrooms. The Reserve is open daily 8 A.M. to dusk.

2. *Mudlick Mill*
This mill was built as a flour mill in 1817, and in 1847 became part of Christian Rohrer's "Mudlick Whiskey Distillery". Although the grounds appear park-like with a covered bridge, pond, and other buildings, it is private property, but can be viewed from the road. (To by-pass the steep hill going west on S.R. 725, go east on S.R. 725, then south on Astoria Road.)

3. *Germantown, Ohio*

4. *Slifer Presbyterian Church and Cemetery*
Built in 1819 as the Union Reformed and Lutheran Church, and since rebuilt twice during the nineteenth century, this attractive church has a working water pump in front, and the old cemetery adjoining the church has gravestones dating back to at least 1815.

5. *Eikenberry-Wheatville Cemetery*
This very early small cemetery has stones dating back to 1811. An interesting tree trunk-shaped marker, placed in 1903 to memorialize one of the area's earliest settlers, bears the inscription "In memory of Peter Eikenberry, born in Germany 1727, emigrated to U.S. about 1750, died in O. 1812."

6. *Route Note*
This section's twisting roads can be rather confusing. Turn left from Sharpsburg onto Aukerman Creek Road. You will make another left from Aukerman Creek onto Brubaker Road, your next left opportunity (it does not cross). There is no sign at Brubaker Road, but you'll see a one-lane bridge sign with a small covered bridge insignia below it a short distance from the intersection. Good luck!

7. *Brubaker Covered Bridge*
This beautiful bridge was built by Everett Sherman in 1887, and was then fully sided. With the coming of the automobile, the sides were opened up to provide better visibility through the sharp curves in and out of the bridge.

8. *Preble County Historical Society—Swartsel Farm*
An early log home, a totem pole, and hiking trails are found here, and the grounds are open daily during daylight hours. On the first Sunday afternoon of the month, you can also tour inside the log home and country store.

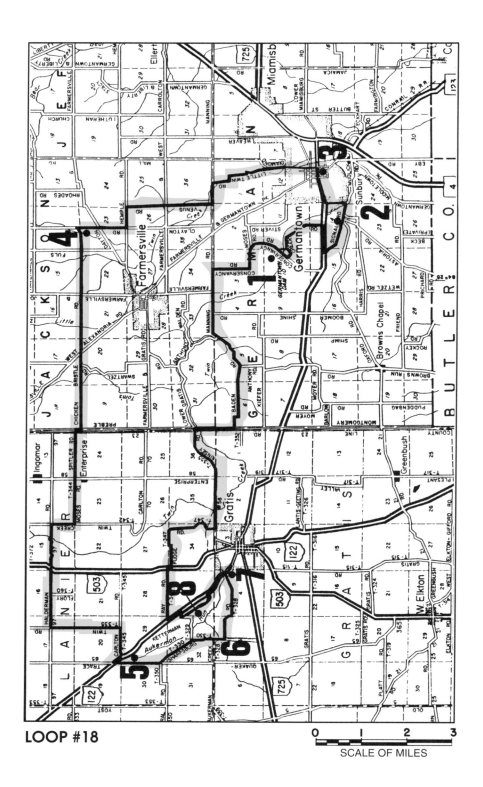

LOOP #18

0   1   2   3

SCALE OF MILES

LOOP #19

Length: 27 miles

Terrain: Rather hilly

County: Greene

Tecumseh and Friend

This beautiful loop takes you over rolling countryside, through pastured farmland, and along lovely streams, into the very heart of the old Shawnee nation in Ohio, as well as into the hearts of its greatest leader and his pioneer friend. The tour is rather hilly in places, and rewards the tourer with panoramic views. Covered bridges, old mills, pioneer cemeteries, a nature preserve, and more are found on this trip.

The Shawnee village of Chalagatha (not to be confused with present day Chillicothe, which was named in honor of the Shawnee village) bustled on the current site of Oldtown, and is the destination of this history-filled ride. Chalagatha was the home of Tecumseh, born in 1768 under a magnificent shooting star. A striking physical figure and born leader, Tecumseh also had the gift of prophecy, and predicted eclipses, earthquakes, and the outcome of great battles. After the defeat of the Indians in 1795, Tecumseh did not participate in the signing of the Greenville Treaty with General Anthony Wayne which pushed the Indians northward. Instead, he began laying the groundwork for uniting all the tribes of North America in a great effort to sweep the settlers back to the eastern sea.

At about this same time, in 1799, James Galloway, a pioneer from Kentucky and Revolutionary War soldier, moved into the valley to establish his home, the first log cabin in the area. As Mr. Galloway and his family were looking over the land, they encountered Tecumseh, and learned that it was Tecumseh's home before the war and treaty pushed him out. Feeling compassion for the displaced warrior, James Galloway told Tecumseh that his door would always be open to him. Thus began one of the few friendships the great Shawnee made with the settlers. So close did Tecumseh and Galloway become that Tecumseh asked for the hand of Galloway's daughter, Rebecca, in marriage. After considerable agonizing on both sides, it was decided that the union could not work in such troubled times. To protect these people that he loved, however, Tecumseh ordered his warriors not to harm women and children when the war came. In 1812 the war did come, and Tecumseh died in battle, serving his people as a British warrior against the Americans.

On this loop, you will find a memorial to Tecumseh, as well as the pioneer cemetery in which James Galloway and his family are buried.

POINTS OF INTEREST:

1. *John Bryan State Park*
   Hiking trails, picnic tables and camping are available at the park.

2. *Grinnell Mill*
   At the bottom of a steep descent is the old Grinnell mill, which is now a private residence.

3. *Grinnell Covered Bridge*
   This bridge, built between 1860 and 1870, formerly stood on Cemetery Road, and was moved to a field just northwest of the old Grinnell mill.

4. *Glen Helen Nature Preserve*
   This nature preserve has beautiful nature trails, the "yellow springs", a swing bridge, and many interesting natural rock formations. The preserve is open during daylight hours, and the trailside museum is open Tues.-Fri. 10-5:30, Sat. & Sun. 12-5:30, closed Mon. To reach the preserve, turn right on Grinnell for 1-1/4 miles, then right on Corry to the entrance.

5. *Stevenson Road Covered Bridge*
   This historic covered bridge, built in 1873, spans Massie Creek.

6. *Oldtown*
   This is the site of the old Shawnee village of Chalagatha. Several stone markers commemorating Tecumseh, Daniel Boone, and Simon Kenton are found here. The markers are located on U.S. 68 about 100 yards south of Brush Row Road.

7. *Stevenson Cemetery*
   In 1804 the Massie Creek Church Lot and Cemetery was established, and is now known as Stevenson Cemetery. This is the pioneer graveyard where James Galloway and his family are

buried, as are many other soldiers of the Revolution. Mr. Galloway's marker indicates that he was "an honest man and pious Christian".

8. **Charleton Mill Covered Bridge**
   This covered bridge was built in 1860, and is located 1/2 mile east on Charleton Mill Road.

9. **Clifton Mill**
   In the village of Clifton stands the Clifton Mill, overlooking the Little Miami River at the head of Clifton Gorge. The mill was established in 1803, the year of Ohio statehood. It was destroyed by fire in the 1840's, and rebuilt in 1869. The mill is water powered by the swift Little Miami River. There are many stone ground products for sale, and an enjoyable little restaurant is also located in the mill. Hours: M-F, 9-6, food 9-3; Sat. & Sun. 8-6, food til 4. Self-guided tours of the mill are offered for a small charge.

10. **Clifton Gorge**
    This nature preserve has hiking trails and lookout points over the gorge. By following the trail a very short distance, you will come to the "Narrows", where Cornelius Darnell, a member of Daniel Boone's party being held captive at Chalagatha, made a daring escape by leaping 22 feet across the gorge to evade his pursuers and flee to Kentucky. The preserve is a National Natural Landmark.

11. **Young's Dairy (Side Trip)**
    This dairy is open 24 hours a day, and has a bakery on the premises. It is one of the few places in Ohio that can sell raw milk, and their ice cream and milk shakes are excellent. You can even pet the cows at this *real* dairy, which is located on the east side of U.S. 68.

12. **Ye Olde Trail Tavern (Side Trip)**
    The tavern is located in Yellow Springs. The village can be reached by taking Route 370 north from John Bryan State Park, then west on Route 343 to U.S. 68, then south into Yellow Springs, a total distance of about 3 miles. The tavern, built in 1827, was the first home in Yellow Springs, then known as Forest Village. The street was originally an Indian trail, and later became part of the stage coach route from Cincinnati to Columbus.

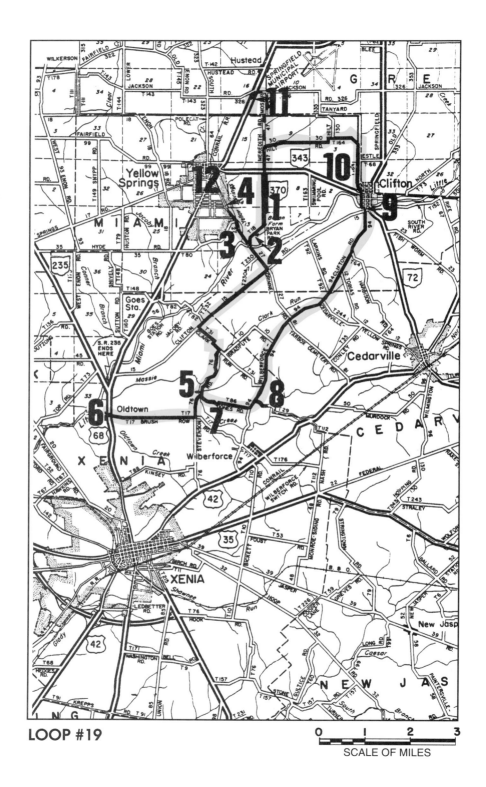

LOOP #19

0   1   2   3

SCALE OF MILES

LOOP #20

Length: 34 miles

Terrain: Rolling to hilly

County: Butler

1812 Ohio

This rolling loop through the countryside of Butler County, Ohio takes the traveler from an 1812 pioneer village to an historic cemetery where veterans of the war of that year are buried, past abandoned one-room schoolhouses and a picturesque ivy-covered stone mill of the mid-nineteenth century, standing at the confluence of two streams, silently guarded by sycamore sentries.

The journey into 1812 is a journey into wilderness in Ohio, a journey made by sturdy individuals, congregations, and even communities. 1812 saw Butler County making advances on the wilderness, as settlements had been established and clearings made in every quarter of the county. Yet, the mighty forest still covered more area than did the cultivated fields, and it was this forest that gave rise to one of the symbols of the early American pioneer, a symbol that came to represent simplicity, strength, and integrity: the log cabin.

The log cabin was the dwelling of the day here at the turn of the nineteenth century. Although humble in appearance, getting such an abode established was a major undertaking, with trees up to three or four feet in diameter needing to be felled to clear a space for the cabin. Once a good spot was selected, preferably near a spring, the first tree was brought down, stripped of its branches, partially squared, and laid on the ground where the cabin would be. Notches were cut into the log near the ends, and other logs were laid into the notches, one at a time, until the cabin reached a sufficient height to be roofed, initially with bark and boughs. Doors were cut in, and windows were made by sawing out about three feet of one of the logs, putting in upright pieces, and pasting paper that had been soaked in bear oil to the uprights. This allowed some light into the quarters, as glass was not readily available or easily transported. The spaces between the logs were filled with mud or

81

clay, and if the settler had not gone mad and fled from the dark forest seeking sunlight and space, he and his family would move into the cabin. As the settler prospered and sawmills were built, the cabin would often be covered with wood siding, but underneath it was unchanged.

The felling of the forest gave the settler both space and material for buildings, and the first log school in the area was built in 1809. But more plentiful than the schools, and more in demand, were the roadside log taverns. A traveler of that time could accomplish only 10-20 miles per day, necessitating frequent overnight accommodations. The smaller log taverns had only a lower room and a loft, into which the traveler ascended by a wooden ladder or stairs. Three or four beds were available in the loft, and if men and women were both using the loft, a curtain was drawn between the sexes. The York shilling, equalling 12-1/2 cents, was used for payment, and a meal might cost one shilling, while sleeping would run to 19 cents. Whiskey and rum cost 3¢ per drink. For the nearby residents, the tavern was more than an overnight stop; it was their social center. While there were no minuets here, there were country reels; no silk or broadcloth, but coarse woolen clothing; no wallflowers, as everyone joined in.

The social scene was not the only difference between the east and the west in 1812; their views of the war also differed. The east viewed it as a war with the British and her navy, while on the frontier it was seen as a battle against the Indians and the British who supported them. Butler County mustered eight companies for the war. Following the American victory in the War of 1812, Britain finally took seriously America's claim to independence, and Tecumseh's death in battle brought a sense of relief to the white settlers along the frontier.

As you follow this route through Butler County, be advised that you will encounter pavement of varying quality. While sufficiently smooth in most places, it is rather rough in others, hinting at another use for logs in the nineteenth century—the log corduroy road.

POINTS OF INTEREST:

1. **Governor Bebb Preserve**
   This 175 acre preserve, operated by the Butler County Park District, is the site of the restored log cabin birthplace of William Bebb, born in 1802, and governor of Ohio 1846-48. It was said that he was a great trial lawyer, as he had the ability to "weep at any time". A number of other nearby log cabins and an early log tavern have been moved here and restored, creating an 1812 village. Tours of the village are conducted on Sundays 1-5, May-Sept. Family camping facilities are available, as are picnic sites and hiking trails.

2. **One-Room Schoolhouse**
   This abandoned brick schoolhouse was built in 1895.

3. **One-Room Schoolhouse**
   Also long abandoned, this brick schoolhouse was constructed in 1881.

4. **Bunker Hill Pioneer Cemetery**
   This historic little cemetery contains the graves of James Deneen, a Revolutionary War veteran and one of the first settlers in the area, Samuel and Elijah Deneen, veterans of the War of 1812, and Jonathon Bressler, a Civil War veteran of the Confederate States of America.

5. **Lanes Mill**
   The first mill on this site was a sawmill and gristmill, established in 1816. This three-story stone mill, long out of service, was built in 1850.

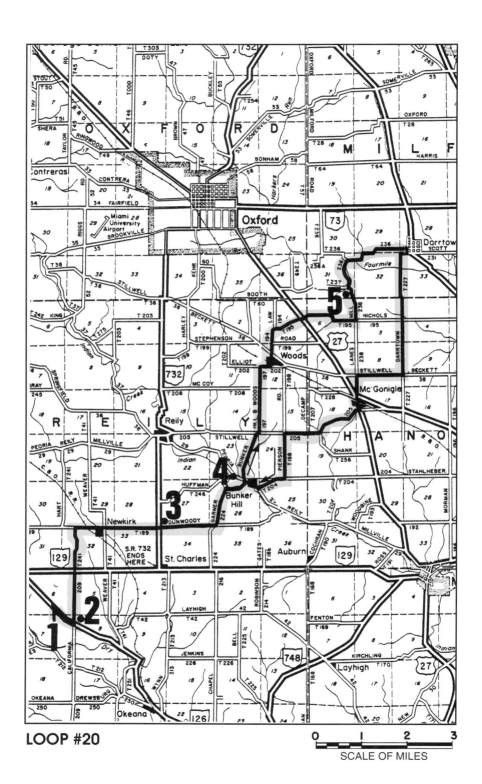

LOOP #20

SCALE OF MILES

0   1   2   3

LOOP #21

Length: 26 miles

Terrain: Flat to hilly

County: Warren

Antiques to Antiquity

The valley of Ohio's first national scenic river, the Little Miami, is the setting of this twenty-six mile riverside ramble in Warren County. Beginning in Waynesville, Ohio, an early Quaker community and present day antique haven, the tour meanders along the sparkling stream, passes an unusual nineteenth century metal bridge, and rises to an ancient hilltop earthworks, making this a ride from antiques to antiquity. A beautiful nature preserve, featuring a deep-cut gorge rich in fossils, is found on the return leg of the loop.

Waynesville, Ohio is a living resource of Quaker history. The area of 4th and High Streets, located "uphill" from Main Street, features the original "White Brick" and "Red Brick" meeting houses, standing opposite each other in both location and doctrine. In 1803, the first twelve families here were granted monthly meeting status, the second such designation in the Northwest Territory. They built the "White Brick" in 1811, which now stands as the oldest Quaker meeting house in continuous service in Ohio. The "Red Brick", today a private residence, was built in 1828 following a schism, and the old cemetery adjoining it was actually rearranged accordingly, with the graves being moved to one end or the other. Stones dating back to 1807 are found in this early cemetery.

From Waynesville, we follow the river back 2,000 years to some of the earliest traces of civilized man in Ohio. Egypt has its pyramids, Greece its Parthenon, and Ohio its earthworks as monuments to ancient times. The early white settlers, trekking into this valley two centuries ago, were mystified by the mounds and earthworks of Fort Ancient. The settlers attributed the mounds to a superior vanished race of men, possibly refugees from Atlantis or the lost tribes of Israel. We now know that these moundbuilders were a highly organized society we call Hopewell Indians, whose culture was centered in southern Ohio from 100 B.C. to 500 A.D. But the mists still swirl around their demise. Why did this society, with a vast trading network stretching for thousands of miles, vanish, leaving southern Ohio virtually unhabited for centuries to come? What cataclysm struck this valley?

As you wander through the hilltop enclosure of Fort Ancient, looking out over the river valley hundreds of feet below, and walk along the four miles of earthen walls surrounding the mounds and crescents within, you will marvel at this astronomical calendar and sanctuary for religious and spiritual events, and ponder the mysterious people of this mystical valley.

POINTS OF INTEREST:

1. *Waynesville, Ohio*

2. *Route Note*
   Be extra cautious, particularly bicyclists, as you travel this short stretch of busy Rt. 42 to the first left.

3. *"Covered" Bridge*
   The date plate on this "covered bridge" reads 1982.

4. *1883 Metal Bridge*
   Lenticular truss bridge afficianados will be delighted to see the only remaining such bridge in Ohio, and the fourth longest of its kind in the United States. It is closed to traffic.

5. *Fort Ancient State Memorial*
   Scenic overlooks, hiking trails, a museum, and picnic tables are features of Fort Ancient, Ohio's first state park. The site is open Memorial Day to Labor Day Wed.-Sunday 10-8, and Apr., May, Oct. weekends, Sat. 10-5, Sun. 12-5. The museum is open summers Wed.-Sat. 10-5, Sun. 12-5. Operated by the Ohio Historical Society, there is a motor vehicle charge.

6. *Caesar Creek Gorge State Nature Preserve*
   This scenic nature preserve along Caesar Creek has restrooms, a parking lot, and a hiking trail. The deep, narrow gorge is rich in fossils, including the trilobite, Ohio's official state fossil. The preserve is open during daylight hours.

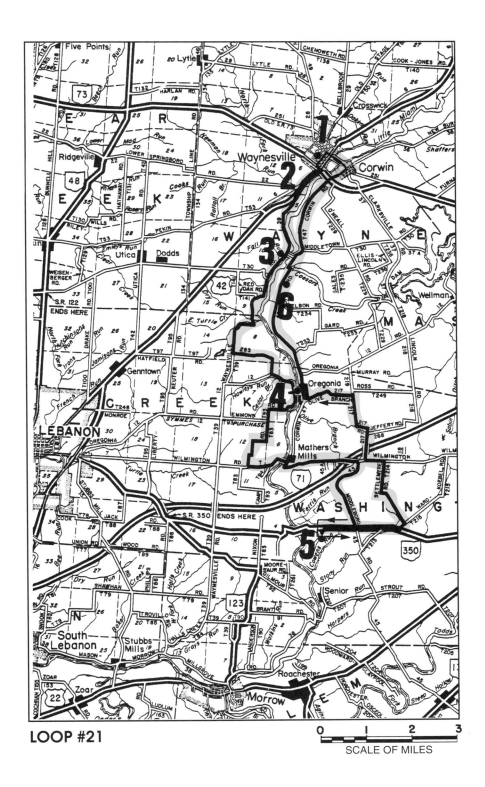

LOOP #21

0   1   2   3

SCALE OF MILES

LOOP #22

Length: 45 miles
(32 miles on short loop)

Terrain: Gently rolling

County: Clinton

Ohio's South Sea

This enchanting tour over the gently rolling hills of Clinton County, Ohio takes the traveler along cascading streams that meander through broad valleys, past wooded ravines, and across ridgetops that provide sweeping views. As you traverse this beautiful countryside, you'll pass through the county's only remaining covered bridge; visit an early pioneer cemetery where Revolutionary War soldiers now rest; and view a magnificent cove abounding in the beautiful American lotus, or water lily. You will also walk along the floor of an ancient Ohio sea.

When one crosses a covered bridge built more than a century ago, it seems from a long ago era—until one visits the banks of Cowan Creek. Here, the realization strikes that all of human history is but an eyeblink in time, a millisecond in the earth's history. The several thousands of years that man has been in Ohio pales before the eons etched in the rocks under our feet along this stream—rocks that are literally older than the hills.

Five-hundred million years ago, Ohio was the floor of a shallow sea, with clear water and warm temperatures resembling that of the Bahamas. This primordial sea gave rise to a vast number of sea creatures long before there were any animals walking the land. Corals, bryozoans, chambered nautiluses, and trilobites, an extinct animal that was destined to become Ohio's official state fossil, lived and died here in southwest Ohio. Through the millenia, the shells of the sea creatures fossilized, and the sea withdrew from Ohio.

Today, along Cowan Creek below the reservoir spillway, the fossils of these ancient animals are so abundant that they literally form the rocks along the banks of the stream. Fossil collectors from all over the world come to marvel at the evidence of a past beyond imagining, for the modern beachcomber of this prehistoric sea can find hundreds of species along the creek banks.

Bicyclists are advised to use caution along the short stretches of state routes. A shortened ride is available by following the short-cut on the map.

POINTS OF INTEREST:

1. **Cowan Creek Fossil Area**
   Parking lots are available by the dam, and the fossil rich creek banks can be reached by crossing Rt. 730 and following a fisherman's trail on the south side of the stream until you reach the creek. Watch your step as you approach the trail, as there is a hidden drain pipe in the grass.

2. **Martinsville Covered Bridge**
   Built in 1871 by Zimri Wall, this is the only remaining covered bridge entirely in Clinton County. A few years after this bridge was completed, Zimri joined with his brother and another man to form the Champion Bridge Co., now known worldwide for its steel products. In 1902, Joe Houk was crossing through the bridge with his large steam engine to thresh wheat at a nearby farm when it crashed through the floor and into the stream. No injuries, but it was quite a job to get the machine out of the creek.

3. **Martinsville, Ohio**
   This tiny community boasts three churches over 100 years old, including the Quaker Church built in 1883, which is beautiful in its simplicity. An early cemetery stands behind the church, and a mysterious monument to "Big Jim, the Great White Hunter" sits at the rear of the cemetery. To take the short-cut from Martinsville, go north on Greene Street. To continue on the main loop, go south on "Cemetry" Road.

4. **1875 Metal Bowstring Bridge**
   This beautiful little bridge, located in an idyllic setting, is unique for its design and wooden deck.

5. **New Antioch Pioneer Cemetery**
   Stones dating back to at least 1822 are found here, including one simply marked "Edward Roberts, a soldier of the revolution". Other Revolutionary War soldiers and Civil War soldiers are also buried here.

6. **Octagonal Barn**
   This rare free-standing octagonal barn was built in 1895. It stands on private property.

7. **Lotus Cove**
   A colony of spectacular water lilies can be seen from the self-guided nature trail here. This is an unusually large colony for an inland lake. The water lily has large, yellow flowers and huge bowl-shaped leaves, and blooms July to September.

8. **Cowan Lake State Park Campground**
   Cabins and Class A camping (showers and flush toilets) are available here. The park also offers a swimming beach.

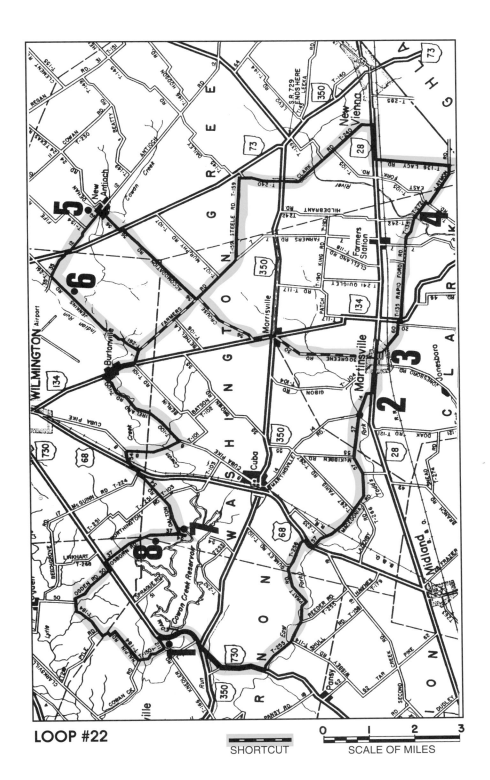

LOOP #22

SHORTCUT

0   1   2   3
SCALE OF MILES

LOOP #23

Length: 31 miles
(18 miles on short loop)

Terrain: Rolling with a few steep hills

County: Clermont/Brown

A Lifetime of Change

This 31 mile tour through the rolling countryside of Clermont and Brown Counties begins at the historic town of Bethel, Ohio, and winds its way through valleys and along ridgetops to one of Ohio's most unique covered bridges, past century-old country churches and by a Civil War era schoolhouse. Sky-blue ponds dot the pastures where horses and ponies frolic, tobacco leaves hang in ramshackle drying barns, and a colony of beautiful water lilies bobs with the gentle waves of Lake Grant.

It was two centuries ago, in 1798, that Obed Denham crossed the Ohio River from slave territory to begin a settlement for people opposed to human slavery. It was still five years until Ohio would become a state, but the Northwest Territory was a free land, and this ardent abolitionist was determined that the entire nation would one day be free. Upon platting Denhamsville, later to be called Bethel, Denham gave two lots for the use of the Regular Baptist Church, "who do not hold slaves or commune at the Lord's table with those who do", to build a church and to bury the dead. This was the first legally organized practical emancipation society west of the Alleghenies. Today, the Early Settlers Burying Ground in Bethel is the final resting place of many of these early Ohio settlers, including Obed Denham, his family, and an "unknown hunter" who was befriended by Denham.

Looking south from the intersection of Main and Plane in Bethel, one can see a two-story red brick house on the west side of the street that was built in 1821-23. It later became the home and office of Dr. Thompson, who died in the 1940's at the age of 104, the oldest practicing physician at that time in the United States. Dr. Thompson saw Ohio change from the canal days of the 1840's, to a highly complex modern society in the span of one lifetime, giving proof to the adage that what one measures in centuries in Europe is measured in decades in America.

As the Thompson boy grew, so did the town and surrounding area. There was much work to be done: bridges needed to be built, schools and churches erected. Dr. Thompson was a young man when the Shiloh schoolhouse was completed in 1866 at the close of the Civil War, and the community took pride in the accomplishment. Through the decades this one-room frame schoolhouse served the township's youngsters and helped give the community its identity. But change is ever in the wind, and when consolidation was sweeping these one-room schoolhouses into a central collection basket, this community fought to keep control of its one-room school. It took the battle to court but lost, and the little schoolhouse closed, the last one-room schoolhouse in the county to do so. Although the little wooden building was built twenty years before the brick one-room schoolhouses that followed, it outlasted them all in serving its original purpose in Brown County, and still stands along this loop today.

Just as the Shiloh schoolhouse is a monument to determination and perseverance, so are the covered bridges found on this tour. The schoolhouse had been standing for a dozen years, and our Dr. Thompson was now in his thirties, when the Brown Covered Bridge was built over Whiteoak Creek in 1878; the doctor was in his fifties, about the halfway point in his life, when the distinctive Newhope Covered Bridge was completed in 1895. The bridges were probably very well-received, as Morgan's Raiders burned two others in the area during their foray into the north during the Civil War. The doctor continued to practice medicine into the mid-twentieth century, while these two old covered bridges survive yet today along the backroads of southwestern Ohio.

Bicyclists are advised that the state routes in and out of Bethel can be rather busy. Route 125 and Route 133 have narrow berms, and extra caution is urged. Cyclists and other travelers who wish to avoid the rather moderate traffic near Bethel, or take a shorter tour, can begin at Lake Grant, and enjoy an 18 mile loop by taking the short-cut north from Neal's Corner and back to Lake Grant.

POINTS OF INTEREST:

1. **Bethel, Ohio/Early Settlers Burying Ground**
   Bethel is the starting point of this tour, and the settlers' burying ground is located on N. Main St. (Route 133) north of Plane St. (Route 125). The stones of three sisters at the front of the cemetery give mute testimony to the scarlet fever outbreak here in 1844. In addition to Obed Denham's grave, those of nineteenth century U.S. Senator Thomas Morris and U.S. Representative Reader Clarke are found here.

2. **Route Note**
   This short stretch of rough pavement is less than 1/4 mile long.

3. **1866 Shiloh Schoolhouse**
   The little school, now used as a meeting room, stands beside a church built in 1877. Aluminum siding has recently been added, covering the original frame structure.

4. **Lake Grant**
   A parking lot is available here for travelers choosing the shorter loop. A colony of American lotus water lilies can be seen from Rt. 774.

5. **Brown Covered Bridge**
   Built in 1878, this timber covered bridge uses the Smith Truss design.

6. **Newhope, Ohio**
   This tiny community is the location of an early brick church built in 1851, an abandoned iron bridge erected in 1884, and one of the smallest town halls in Ohio.

7. **Newhope Covered Bridge**
   One must stop and walk into this old bridge, now closed to traffic, to appreciate its distinctiveness. Massive arches consisting of eleven boards bolted together run along the sides and extend down to the abutments. This Burr arch bridge was built in 1895.

8. **Mt. Nebo Methodist Church**
   The date plate on this country church indicates that it was originally constructed in 1835.

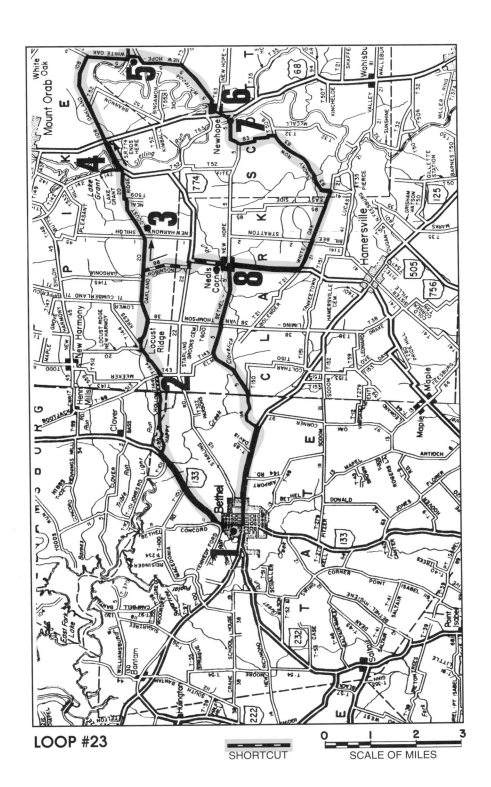

LOOP #23

SHORTCUT

0   1   2   3

SCALE OF MILES

SECTION III. *Northwest Ohio*

One room schoolhouse

Trip Planning Guide
Northwest Ohio

# Name	Length (miles) short loop	Historical site	Nature preserve	Museum	Covered bridge	Pioneer cemetery	Picnic area	Camping (state/county park)	Swimming	Walking trails
24. Magnificent Metal	29	X		X	X	X	X			X
*25. Down By The Old Mill Stream	45 (30)	X		X		X	X	X		X
*26. The Andrews Raiders Tour	25	X				X	X	X	X	X
27. The Crane Creek Tour	39	X	X			X	X		X	X
28. The Tarhe Trek	48	X	X	X	X	X	X			X
29. The Black Swamp Tour	48	X	X			X	X	X		X
30. The Great Northwest Tour	47 (31)	X				X	X	X	X	X
31. Island of Stone	14	X	X	X		X		X	X	
32. The Road to Recovery	45	X		X			X			
*33. Top of the Canal	21	X		X			X	X	X	
*34. The Fort Amanda Tour	42	X				X	X	X	X	X
35. Red Barn Country	31	X		X		X	X			X

* Camp-Over Option: <u>Two</u> loops leave from same state park where camping is available.

Tour Loop Locations
Northwest Ohio

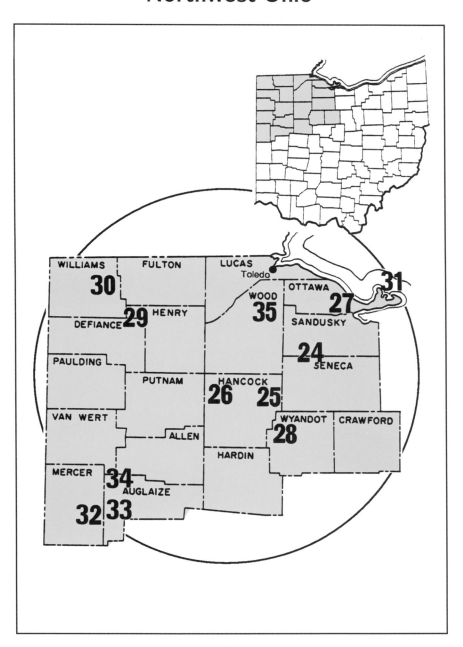

LOOP #24

Length: 29 miles

Terrain: Flat to gently rolling

County: Sandusky/Seneca

Magnificent Metal

This 29 mile tour through the flat to gently rolling countryside of Sandusky and Seneca Counties begins along the banks of the scenic Sandusky River, winds past historic sites from the War of 1812, passes beautiful country churches, and takes the traveler across river and stream on a variety of bridges, including covered and iron spans. The route then departs from the river to cross open countryside on the way to "the world's largest natural sulphur springs".

There is a certain charm, an allure, to the majestic bridges of days gone by. The importance of a bridge to a young community striving for growth is displayed in the scale and pride with which the early bridge builders plied their craft. Far from making a bridge virtually indistinguishable from the roadway, yesteryear's engineers and ironworkers made monuments to their skills, creating structures that towered above their surroundings. With their beams arching high overhead in a constellation of iron, the river rushing beneath in full view, it is an event to cross these wonderful old spans.

The importance of these bridges, whether they be of iron or timber, is reflected not only in their size and scale, but in the struggles that underlie many of them. One bridge on this loop, the Abbott Bridge, is on a site steeped in controversy and tragedy. In 1870, the first bridge built on this site, the Watson Bridge, was erected over the objections of the people of Fort Seneca, who wanted a bridge over the Sandusky River located closer to them. Watson, being a county commissioner, got his way, but an early account reveals that "the bridge was more an experiment than a good job. The timbers were left exposed, and the bridge was not anchored well. When the great hurricane swept over the northern part of Seneca County in June, 1875, blew down the M.E. Church in Fort Seneca, throwing it flat on the ground, it also blew the Watson Bridge into the river in a body, leaving the abutments only".

100

After the "hurricane", the haggling began again, and while the bickering continued, two men drowned trying to cross the river to vote in a township election. It was then decided to build the new bridge at Fort Seneca. A few years later, a Mr. Flummerfelt persuaded the commissioners to put up some money, along with his, and the Flummerfelt Covered Bridge was erected on the site of the Old Watson Bridge, followed in 1897 by the metal bridge that stands yet today.

Although the metal bridges of the late nineteenth century are now vanishing, the traveler on this loop will pass an even earlier bridge over the East Branch of Wolf Creek. Built in 1851, the Mull Covered Bridge has earned a place on the National Register of Historic Places. By-passed and preserved, the bridge is one of the backroad treasures of Sandusky County.

POINTS OF INTEREST:

1. **Wolf Creek Park**
   The loop begins at Sandusky County's Wolf Creek Park, nestled along the west bank of the scenic Sandusky River on the east side of SR 53. Picnic tables, restroom facilities, grills, drinking water, and nature trails are available, and a camping area is located about one mile south of the park.

2. **Caution: Route Note**
   Be extra cautious as you travel busy SR 53. A narrow berm is available for cyclists.

3. **Hill Cemetery**
   Located on the northeast corner of SR 53 and TR 9 is an early cemetery where the grave markers of John Delong and Jacob King, veterans of the War of 1812, can be found.

4. **Mull Covered Bridge**
   Spanning the East Branch of Wolf Creek on TR 9 is the by-passed Mull Covered Bridge. Built in 1851, this Howe Truss bridge is on the National Register of Historic Places. Photographers may want to take advantage of the view from the replacement parallel bridge.

5. **1875 M.E. Church**
   When "the great hurricane of 1875" destroyed the M.E. Church, "throwing it flat on the ground", this beautiful church was built in its place. The church has not been used since 1975, and now is private property. It is clearly visible from the road as you pass by.

6. **Fort Seneca Bridge**
   This strikingly beautiful bridge was built in 1914, and spans the Sandusky River on TR 143.

7. **Abbott's Bridge**
   Water and latrines are available at the far end of the bridge.

8. **1879 Church & Pleasant Union Cemetery**
   Elegant in its simplicity, this white frame country church stands across the road from the ornately fenced Pleasant Union Cemetery. The cemetery is home to a large war memorial to Americans who have died in war from the Revolution to Viet Nam, Gettysburg to Shiloh.

9. **Old Fort, Ohio**
   Although the nearby community of Fort Seneca has the name, the actual site of the now vanished fort was at present day Old Fort, Ohio. As you approach the town on CR 51, keep an eye out for the stone tablet at CR 51 and Harrison Street that marks the spot of William Henry Harrison's 1813 Fort Seneca. It was on this spot that General Harrison received from Commodore Perry the famous message "We have met the enemy and they are ours".

10. **1924 Metal Bridge**

11. **Green Springs, Ohio**
    Home of the "world's largest natural sulphur springs", people would travel great distances to this one-time resort seeking the healing properties of the water. The Seneca Indians also were aware of the unusual properties of the waters, and attempted to choke off the springs when they were forced from the area in 1814. The springs can be found in the idyllic park-like setting of the St. Francis complex on the north edge of town. The park is open daily to the public, and can be entered at the north gate.

12. **Decker Cemetery**
    In this windblown cemetery that stands alone in a farm field just north of TR 173 on CR 53 are buried three veterans of the War of 1812.

13. **Gilmore Bridge**
    The two spans of the Gilmore Bridge over the Sandusky River, while still standing, are no longer open to vehicular traffic.

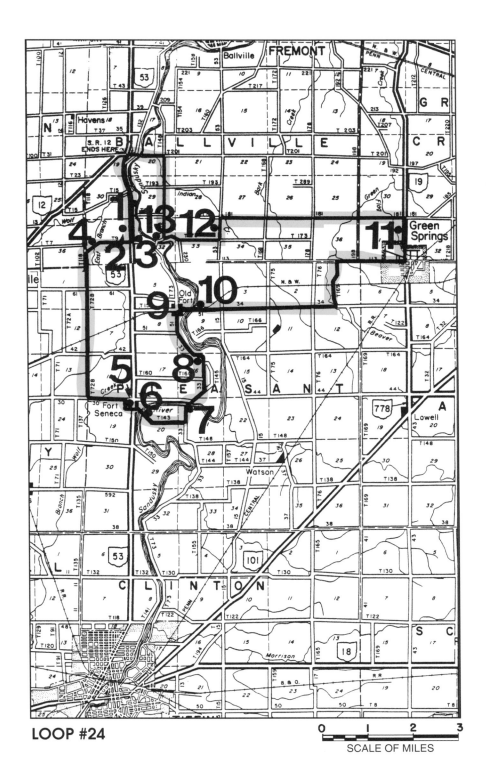

LOOP #24

0   1   2   3

SCALE OF MILES

LOOP #25

Length: 45/30 miles

Terrain: Flat to gently rolling

County: Hancock

Down By The Old Mill Stream

This loop, one of two from Van Buren State Park, traverses the open countryside of Hancock County, skirts the eastern fringe of Findlay, then winds along the banks of the Blanchard River before circling northward again through open countryside. Along the way are one room schoolhouses, ornate iron bridges, parks, and beautiful country houses, dotting the landscape through which flows one of the most sung about streams in the world.

A century and a half ago, in the year 1835, Michael Misamore built a mill, the first frame structure in Amanda Township, Hancock County, Ohio, along the banks of the beautiful Blanchard River. The mill was run by water power, which was described in an early history book as "uncertain, through freezing in winter and low water in summer. Nevertheless, it was a great boon to the pioneers of the surrounding country, who often had to travel long distances through forest, with a small grist, ere the little ones could taste the luxury of a wheat cake."

While providing the little ones a taste of a wheat cake was the mill's main purpose, romance proved to be a more lasting product. In 1910, Tell Taylor was inspired to write of the mill on the Blanchard River one of the most famous songs of all time, "Down by the Old Mill Stream". Taylor, born on a farm near Vanlue and reared and educated in Findlay, moved to New York in 1897 and, with two other men, opened one of the first publishing houses on Tin Pan Alley. It was on a return visit to Hancock County in 1908 that he wrote the famous song. Taylor returned to Findlay for good in 1922, and is buried in a cemetery near Vanlue, along the river that he loved and made famous. "The old mill wheel is silent, and has fallen down", wrote Taylor, and today there is no trace left at all of the mill. However, the stream that gave rise to the mill and inspired the song is still meandering through the countryside of Hancock County, Ohio, flowing beneath the beautiful bridges of Tell Taylor's day, compelling us to slow our pace, if only for a little while, down by the old mill stream.

For travelers desiring a shorter loop, a 30 mile ride is provided by taking the short cut indicated on the map after your visit to Riverbend Park. Those opting for the shorter loop, however, forfeit the right to sing "Down By The Old Mill Stream" in rounds as they head back into the wind to Van Buren State Park.

Campers are advised that another day of exploring is available with "The Andrews Raiders Tour", also departing from Van Buren State Park.

POINTS OF INTEREST:

1. **Van Buren State Park**
   The tour begins in Van Buren State Park, a small park located east of the railroad tracks and south of TR 218. The park offers camping (no electricity, vault toilets), picnicking, and a shelterhouse.

2. **The Little Red Schoolhouse**
   This charming 1850's schoolhouse, complete with privies and pump, has been restored inside and out by the Hancock County Retired Teachers Association and the Hancock Historical Museum. Hours are by appointment.

3. **The Blanchard River: The Old Mill Stream**
   A winding little road, TR 208, follows the beloved river that is immortalized in Tell Taylor's "Down By The Old Mill Stream". This scenic stretch is only a few miles downstream from the spot of the old mill he described. Ironically, the river was earlier called "Tailor's River" by the Indians after the tailor Blanchard.

4. **Riverbend Park**
   The route passes through Hancock County's Riverbend Park, where drinking water, latrines, and picnic facilities are available.

5. **Reservoir Overlook**
   For travelers feeling the need for a little extra exertion, a hike up the earthen levee of the Findlay Reservoir may provide a glimpse of waterfowl on the man-made lake.

6. **1879 Metal Bridge**
   This beautiful bridge over the Blanchard River on TR 207 was constructed in 1879 by the Columbia Bridge Works of Dayton, Ohio. After crossing the bridge, make a right turn onto TR 244.

7. *1876 Metal Bridge*
   Located just west of the loop on TR 205 is another ornate metal bridge, this one constructed by the Wrought Iron Bridge Company of Canton, Ohio.

8. *One Room Schoolhouse*
   Located just east of the loop on TR 205 is a one room school-house from 1889, used more recently as the Riverside Grange.

9. *Route Note:* Hazardous crossing of SR 15.

10. *Van Horn Cemetery*
    Here, in the center of this little cemetery, nestled between two small shrubs, is the grave marker of Tell Taylor, 1876-1937, that reads "author-composer-publisher, whose inspired song 'Down By The Old Mill Stream' continues to give pleasure to millions and to endear his memory in the hearts of his friends and neighbors of Hancock County". Upon leaving the cemetery, make a right jog to follow TR 190.

11. *Misamore Mill Site*
    Mill stream devotees can stand on the bridge on CR 169 just west of the loop and look north to the east bank where the famed mill once stood along the Blanchard River.

12. *1885 Schoolhouse*
    Here is yet another of the century-old former schoolhouses that dot the countryside of rural Ohio.

13. *Vanlue, Ohio*
    Tell Taylor was born in Vanlue in 1876. Follow SR 330 through the village, north to TR 175.

14. *1888 Enon Valley Presbyterian Church*
    In front of the church is the 100 year old church bell, and the little cemetery beside the church is the resting place of at least two early American veterans. Use extra caution along the one-quarter mile stretch of busy U.S. 224 if visiting the church.

15. *Arcadia Community Park*
    Picnicking areas are available in this community park, located just northwest of SR 12.

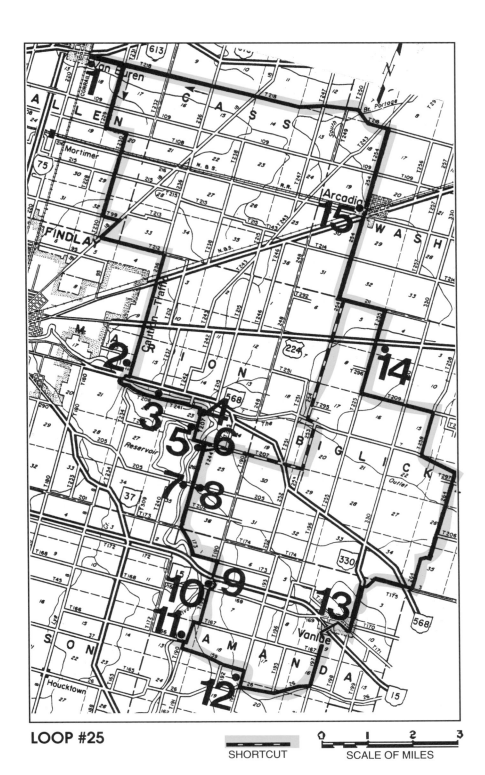

LOOP #25

SHORTCUT

SCALE OF MILES

0 1 2 3

LOOP #26

Length: *25 miles*

Terrain: *Flat*

County: *Hancock*

The Andrews Raiders Tour

"God loves Ohio or he would not have given her such a galaxy of heroes to defend the nation in its hour of trial."
— Rutherford B. Hayes
U.S. President 1877-81

Hancock County has been described by cyclists as one giant bikeway, and indeed, the sparsely traveled lanes that stretch between rows of corn and wheat often seem to be ideal bike paths, although they are actually county and township roads. Cyclists and other backroad buffs will delight in traveling through this checkerboard of emerald and gold that is home to productive farms, small towns, and a pride and heritage that runs back to the Civil War. This ride, one of two from Van Buren State Park, takes the traveler back in time to one of the most daring episodes of the entire War Between the States.

Ohio gave the country Generals Grant, Sherman, and Sheridan, and she also gave more of her sons to the Union Army than any other state, a fact that is poignantly visible with a walk through the early cemeteries along this loop. The little metal G.A.R. markers that attend so many gravestones silently attest to the service of more than half of the state's adult male population to the "Grand Army of the Republic". And on a grander scale, a large memorial to one of the most heroic adventures of the entire war can be found on this tour, a statue and historical marker to the famous Andrews Raiders.

On April 12, 1862, at Big Shanty, Georgia, a raid began that was to capture the imagination of the nation and live on in books and movies, including Walt Disney's "The Great Locomotive Chase". Twenty-two soldiers from the North, mostly Ohioans, had penetrated into northern Georgia, intent on stealing a locomotive and then using it to burn bridges behind them as they made a run for the north. When the crew from the Con-

108

federate locomotive "The General" detrained to eat breakfast, the raiders seized the train and took off north, attempting to destroy the confederate supply lines. Pursuit began immediately, and the great chase did not end until 90 miles later, when the locomotive ran out of fuel and the soldiers were forced to abandon the train. All were captured, and eight of the men were executed for the deed at Atlanta in June, 1862. Eight others escaped confinement, and the remaining Raiders were later paroled. All the participants were awarded the Congressional Medal of Honor, the first recipients of this distinguished honor. In 1891, the state of Ohio erected a monument to the Andrews Raiders in the National Cemetery at Chatanooga, the site of the graves of those executed.

Closer to home, travelers along this Hancock County loop can visit the graves of John R. Porter and William Bensinger, two of the Andrews Raiders buried in their home state of Ohio. Porter was one of the men who escaped from confinement, and Bensinger was exchanged to the North almost a year later. Captain Bensinger's Medal of Honor can be seen at the McComb Library as you pass through town. Following your visit to the library, you may want to stop for a picnic lunch at the community park before heading back through the open countryside to Van Buren State Park.

Campers are advised that another day of exploring is available with the "Down By The Old Mill Stream Tour", also departing from Van Buren State Park.

POINTS OF INTEREST:

1. **Van Buren State Park**
   Located just east of the railroad tracks and south of TR 218, this small state park offers no-frills camping, picnicking, and a shelterhouse. Exit the park and follow SR 613 (Market St.) through town.

2. **Van Buren, Ohio**
   You will see a historical marker in the village square describing the history of the town, which was laid out in 1833. It is named for Martin Van Buren, U.S. President from 1837-41.

3. *Thomas Cemetery*

Located at the northeast corner of CR 203 and TR 134, this little cemetery contains the graves of about a dozen Civil War veterans, and one veteran of the War of 1812.

4. *Union Cemetery*

Located just west on Main Street (SR 613) from CR 126, McComb's Union Cemetery is home to an impressive memorial to "Our Honored Dead 1861-1865". The likeness of a Civil War soldier faces south from the top of the monument. Located by the monument is a historical marker to the Andrews' Raiders, including William Bensinger and John R. Porter. Bensinger is buried due south of the monument toward the road, and Porter's grave is located about a dozen rows west of Bensinger's.

5. *McComb, Ohio*

From the cemetery, travel east on SR 613 (Main St.) through the town of McComb, the second largest community in Hancock County. William Bensinger's Congressional Medal of Honor can be seen at the McComb Library, 113 S. Todd St.

6. *Cloe Greiner Memorial Park*

A historical marker for the village of McComb can be found beside an early crude log structure in the park. Picnicking facilities, water, and latrines are located here, as is a swimming pool (admission charge for the pool). To reach the park, go south on SR 186 to the edge of town. The park is on the east side of the road.

7. *Pleasant Hill Cemetery*

On the south side of CR 109 east of CR 139 is the Pleasant Hill Cemetery, where the markers of many Civil War veterans, and at least one veteran of the War of 1812, can be found.

8. *Route Note*

CR 220 into Van Buren is rather busy, so use extra caution. A berm is available for cyclists.

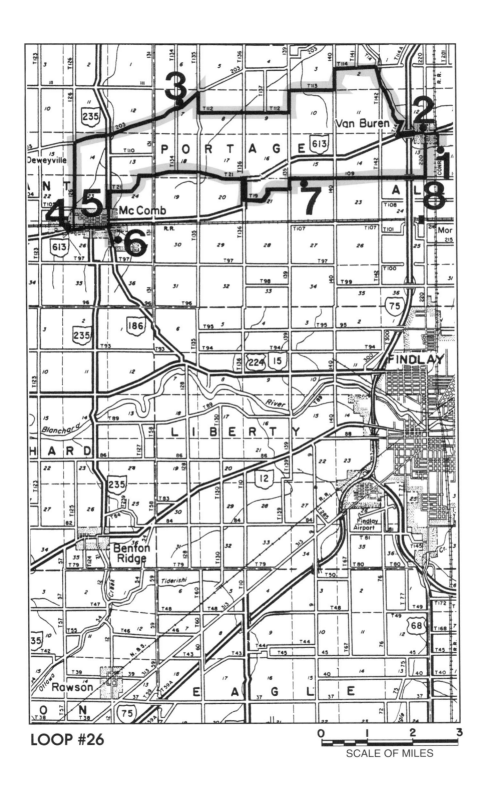

LOOP #26

0   1   2   3
SCALE OF MILES

LOOP #27

Length: 39 miles

Terrain: Mostly flat

County: Ottawa/Lucas

The Crane Creek Tour

Whether your interest is natural history, American history, or simply a riverside ramble through the countryside, this Ottawa County loop, covering 39 miles from the western shore of Lake Erie inland to Genoa, Ohio, offers something for almost every backroad explorer. You may want to begin your trek with an early morning birdwalk through the Magee Marsh, followed by a ride along the Portage River to Elmore, where you can visit the graves of two veterans of the Revolutionary War. After a picnic in a riverside park in Elmore, you'll pass through the town of Genoa, with its shrine, historic outhouse and town hall/opera house, before winding your way to the Ottawa National Wildlife Refuge and an opportunity to see what most Americans have never seen in the wild—the bald eagle. A refreshing swim at the sand beach at Crane Creek finishes off a full day of exploring.

Magee Marsh, a rare example of wild marshland, is known to Ohio birders as the Mecca of Migration, attracting migrating warblers and their watchers every Spring and Fall. Waterfowl are abundant in the preserve, as are other forms of wildlife, including muskrats, foxes, raccoons, and minks. Teeming with life, this treasure along the lake is adjacent to Crane Creek State Park, which offers parking, swimming, and picnic facilities.

Rich not only in natural history, Ottawa County is home to three veterans of the Revolutionary War, and your visit to Elmore will take you to the graves of two of these earliest American veterans, John Green and Israel Harrington. Standing by the simple grave markers of these men, one can feel a connection to the events of Concord and Lexington, Boston and Philadelphia, and imagine the trials and triumphs these men experienced under the command of General George Washington.

From Elmore to Genoa, we shift gears to visit a famous shrine, the Lourdes Grotto, as well as two sites on the National Register of Historic Places, the Town Hall/Opera House and the famous

112

outhouse. The Town Hall was built in 1885, and the Opera House, located on the second floor, was built the following year. The Hall was used not only for theater, but for the yearly caucuses, Medicine Shows, and even a coroner's inquest of the town's first murder. Placed on the National Register of Historic Places in 1976, the Hall earned a place in Chesley's Collection of Historic Theatres in 1983.

Less imposing, but also on the National Register, is the privy on the grounds of the Camper Elementary School, one of the last of its kind. Built in 1870, this elegant brick outhouse, if located away from the school on a country road, could easily be mistaken for a little one-room schoolhouse, as it is built along the same lines.

Near the end of your travels, you'll pass the Ottawa National Wildlife Refuge. In the days when John Green and Israel Harrington were fighting for independence, the bald eagle, our national symbol, was abundant along the shores of Lake Erie. But as their habitat disappeared and pesticides weakened their egg shells, they became an endangered species. By 1975, only four active eagle nests remained in Ohio. The eagle is now making a comeback, and Ottawa Refuge is considered one of the best places in the Midwest to see these raptors. You may wish to stop here for a visit before taking that plunge into Lake Erie at the beach at Crane Creek State Park.

POINTS OF INTEREST:

1. *Crane Creek State Park*
   The tour begins at Crane Creek State Park, where a parking lot, swimming beach, and picnic facilities are available.

2. *Magee Marsh Wildlife Area*
   This superb wildlife area is located adjacent to Crane Creek State Park. Wildlife and birdlife abound along the nature trails that wind along the levees. The trails begin at the beach parking lot. Observation towers and displays are located at the Wildlife Experiment Station on the park road as you leave the park. Hours for the Station are 8-5 M-F, and summer Saturdays 8:30-5, summer Sundays 12-6.

3. *Route Note*
   SR 2, the only road to the refuge, is very busy, and on summer weekends, also carries Cedar Point bound travelers. A narrow

berm is available, and the distance is only about one-half mile each way. Nevertheless, persons choosing to travel by bicycle are advised that it is a hazardous road, and extra caution is advised.

4. **Harris-Elmore Union Cemetery**
   John Green, a soldier of the Revolutionary War, is buried in this cemetery. To reach the cemetery, turn south on Schultz-Portage Road. Enter the second drive into the cemetery, and you'll find Mr. Green's marker by the flag pole, about eight rows south of the drive. Following your visit, return to Portage River South Rd.

5. **Harrington Cemetery**
   This very old, well maintained cemetery, surrounded by an iron fence, is the last resting place of Israel Harrington, another veteran of the Revolutionary War. His marker reads "Pvt., Allen's Vermont Militia, Revolutionary War, died Sept. 10, 1825." Beside his marker is a marker to his son and namesake, "Judge, First Trustee, First Minister U.B. Sandusky Circuit, 1830." The cemetery is located on the north side of Rice St. (Portage River South Rd.) as you enter Elmore.

6. **Elmore, Ohio**
   For travelers wishing to stop for a picnic, two options are available in Elmore. The Walter Ory Park is located just off the loop on the south side of Rice St. about two blocks beyond Toledo Street. Picnic tables, drinking water, a restored train depot and log house are found in the park. A riverside park with picnic tables is available on the loop just after your turn onto SR 51 (Toledo St.). To continue on the loop, take SR 51 (Toledo St.) over the river to CR 213.

7. **Genoa, Ohio**
   History buffs will delight in a ride down Main Street (CR 51). After entering the town, you'll see the fascinating Lourdes Grotto on the west side of the street. The famous privy of the Camper Elementary School is just north of the Grotto, and Genoa's Town Hall/Opera House is on the east side of Main Street in the center of town. At SR 51, make a right to Holts East Rd. (T40), then left.

8. **Ottawa National Wildlife Refuge**
   The refuge is open sunrise to sunset, year round. Nature trails are provided through the refuge.

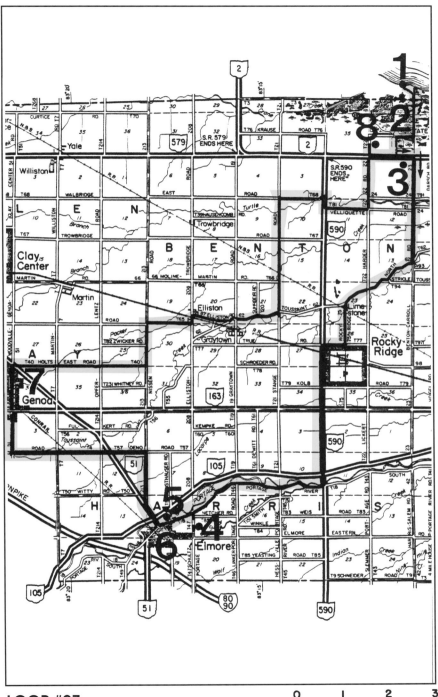

LOOP #27

0 1 2 3

SCALE OF MILES

Length: 48 miles

Terrain: Flat to rolling, with a few hills

County: Wyandot/Seneca/Hancock

The Tarhe Trek

This lovely tour through the northwest quarter of Wyandot County begins with a visit to the Ice Age, then takes us through two centuries of strife and settlement in Northwest Ohio. Along the way are the signposts of the settlers, the old cemeteries, country churches, one room schoolhouses, a covered bridge, and an old mill. A memorial to a great Indian chief and a marker to a battle between the Indians and the army stand mutely along these backroads, reminding us of the price paid for this soil. Deeds of honor and deeds of horror all took place in this gently rolling countryside, seen from these ridgetops today as a panorama of beautiful farms and farmhouses.

So rich is the Indian history in Wyandot County that the county takes its very name from one of the dominant tribes here in the eighteenth century. Several Indian villages were located along the San-doo-stee River (later mistakenly called "San-dusky"), including Cranetown, home of one of the greatest Indian chiefs in the Ohio Country. Tarhe, the Crane, was behind only Little Turtle and Blue Jacket in command of the Indian forces that amassed to fight the Indian Wars of the 1790's, and these forces defeated the American Army twice before finally falling to General "Mad" Anthony Wayne. And it was Tarhe, chief of the Wyandots, who was given the wampum belt of peace on behalf of the Indian tribes by Anthony Wayne at the signing of the Treaty of Greenville in 1795.

In 1811, in the face of pressure from Tecumseh to join in the great uprising, Tarhe declared that he still held high the "wide white wampum of peace", and would not again wage war against the Americans. Two years later, when the United States was at war with Great Britain and Tecumseh's federation of tribes, William Henry Harrison appealed for help from the neutral tribes. Tarhe responded, "We have been waiting many moons for an invitation to fight for the Americans. I speak on behalf of all the tribes present when I profess our friendship. We have agreed, without any dissension, to join you." Today, along a little country road, the backroad explorer will find a marker, nearly obscured by bushes, that reads simply, "Distinguished Wyandot Chief and Loyal American, Tarhe, died here in Cranetown in 1818".

It was in the same year of Tarhe's passing that the United States government gave 16,000 acres of land here to the Wyandot Indians. The land, being wet and marshy, was unsuitable for agriculture, but was excellent for hunting and trapping. Fed by cool, calcium-rich springs, the marshes supported a wide variety of plant and animal life, with several species dating back to the Ice Age. Now the largest remaining inland wetland in this part of the state, travelers can visit this prehistoric remnant at Springville Marsh and stroll along the boardwalk observing nature's bounty.

One other event commemorated the loyalty of the Wyandots during the War of 1812, the giving of Indian Mill to the Indians for their use in grinding wheat into flour. Near the site of that mill is the Indian Mill State Memorial, the nation's first museum of milling in an original mill. You can tour the mill, then take a refreshing break across the river at a scenic park and picnic spot, which is also the ideal location for taking photographs of the picturesque old mill.

POINTS OF INTEREST:

1. *Carey, Ohio*
   The tour begins near Carey, and bicyclists may want to park in the village and travel SR 199 north to T5 to join the loop. As always, extra caution is advised along state routes. A narrow berm is available for cyclists along SR 199. Food and drink are available in the town.

2. *Springville Marsh State Nature Preserve*
   Located on the south side of T24, visitors can stroll through the marsh on a boardwalk, and use the observation tower to spot the wildlife that abounds here.

3. *1878 German Baptist Church*
   Now the Oak Grove Church of the Brethren, this country church was built more than a century ago by German settlers. It is located on the southwest corner of T206 and T266.

4. Lutheran Ridge Cemetery

This early cemetery straddles T95 just inside Wyandot County. Stones dating back to at least 1839 can be found here, as can several markers bearing interesting inscriptions and artwork. One marker, from 1864, testifies that the man was a member of the Ohio National Guard.

5. Caution: Hazardous Crossing of SR 15

6. 1894 Schoolhouse

This abandoned one-room schoolhouse at C96 and T42 is unusual in that it still boasts the old bell tower, sans bell, that would summon the children to class from the surrounding countryside.

7. St. Joseph's Catholic Church

This magnificent brick country church looms above the fields as you approach it along C103.

8. North Salem Lutheran Church

This church, altered in 1972, was originally built in 1850. A walk through the adjacent cemetery reveals a number of early markers, including many written in German.

9. Caution: Hazardous Crossing of SR 23

10. Wyandott Indian Mission (side trip)

The restored mission, the first Methodist mission in America, can be visited by traveling south on busy SR 53 1.8 miles to E. Church St., then left 1-1/2 blocks. It was founded by John Stuart in 1816. Services are held in the mission on summer Sundays at 8:00 A.M. Just southwest of the mission, along the walk, is the grave marker of Christianna Haag, who died "Feb. 31, 1862."

11. Battle Island Monument

Located at the intersection of SR 67 and C47 is a marker commemorating the defeat of Colonel William Crawford at Battle Island in 1782. It was here that the Indians wreaked a terrible vengeance on Crawford for the earlier massacre of the Moravian Indians at Gnadenhutten. Crawford was not responsible for the massacre, but his associate, David Williamson, who fled, was. The torture that the tribes had planned for Williamson was exacted on Crawford in his place. Although called Battle Island, the battle took place here, and not on an island.

12. **Indian Mill**

Located by a large metal bridge where C47 crosses the Sandusky River, the mill is now a museum of milling, operated by the
Ohio Historical Society. Hours of operation are Fri.-Sat. 9:00-5,
Sun. 1-6, June through October. Admission charge. Across the
river from the mill is a park and picnic area with restrooms, and a
display of the millstones used by the Wyandots before Indian Mill
was constructed.

13. **Parker Covered Bridge**

Built in 1873 by J.C. Davis, this Howe Truss covered bridge spans
the Sandusky River on T40. It is one of only two covered bridges
still in use in the county.

14. **Tarhe Monument**

Located left about one-half mile on C37, travelers can visit this
modest memorial to the great Wyandot chief.

15. **Caution: Route Note**

Use extra caution as you travel this short stretch of SR 53.

16. **Cemetery**

An early cemetery can be found just beyond the turn from 105
to T11.

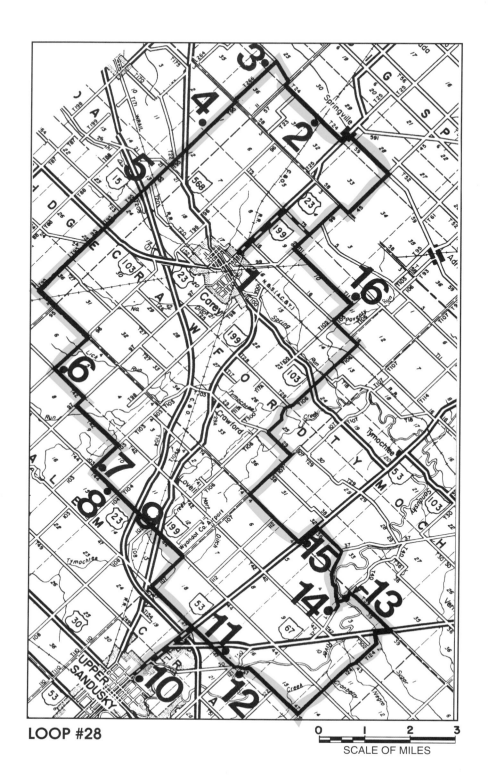

LOOP #28

SCALE OF MILES

0　1　2　3

LOOP #29

Length: 48 miles

Terrain: Flat

County: Defiance/Henry/Fulton

The Black Swamp Tour

This country tour over the rich, flat farmland of northwest Ohio begins along the banks of the beautiful Maumee River, then crosses open countryside on a journey back in time, passing through a time tunnel of trees before re-emerging to curve gently along country roads past beautiful red barns, one room schoolhouses, and country churches. "It is an interesting country to travel through", wrote historian Henry Howe in 1849. And nearly a century and a half later, it remains so.

"A greater part of this country is covered by the famous Black Swamp, sustaining a magnificent forest almost impene-trable to the rays of the sun", wrote Howe. While the pioneers virtually wiped out the great forest, travelers along this loop today can look back in time and see a rare reminder of this magnificent woodland at Goll Woods, an essentially virgin wood-lot that survived the ages thanks to the Goll family's love of their "Big Woods". Peter Goll, Sr., his wife Catherine, and son Peter Jr. came from Dobs, France in 1836. They were farmers, but they also loved the trees, and for four generations the Goll family resisted the efforts of the timber operators. In 1966 the land was acquired by the State of Ohio as the last remnant of primeval forest in northwest Ohio. Trees dating back more than five centuries still live here, stretching their branches to the sky more than one-hundred feet above the woodland floor. In spring, a carpet of wildflowers races to blossom before the budding leaves above shut out the sunshine until winter; in summer, the traveler will find respite from the heat of the surrounding country-side in this island of trees, and in fall, the magnificence of the woods is unsurpassed.

The Great Black Swamp, a Connecticut-sized legacy of an earlier and larger Lake Erie, slowed settlement in northwest Ohio, but an undertaking of Herculean proportions conquered the swamp and brought settlers and agriculture to the region. The markers of this triumph, considered one of the greatest such efforts in the world, attract virtually no attention from the traveler rushing by them today, but the huge roadside ditches along these country roads are indeed historic. More than 125 years ago, industrious German pioneer families began digging ditches to drain the swamp, and our friend Howe noted prophetically at the time that "probably, in less than a century, when it shall be cleared and drained, it will be the garden of Ohio, and support half a million people". When the area was drained, land values shot up from $2.00 per acre to $10.00 per acre, and today, while the area accounts for only 11% of the state's land, it provides 25% of the state's agricultural income.

While the roadside ditches were used to carry water away from the fields, another ditch was being dug at about the same time to bring water through the area. The Miami and Erie Canal, called by many the "Big Ditch", connected the Ohio River and Lake Erie, providing access to the larger markets for the farmers of the region. A six mile long stretch of the old canal still survives along the Maumee River at Independence Dam State Park, and hikers can walk along the old towpath where the mules trod over a century ago. With the old canal, the big woods, and the scattering of old schoolhouses and churches, this area truly remains "an interesting country to travel through".

POINTS OF INTEREST:

1. **Independence Dam State Park**
   Located off SR 424 between the Maumee River and the Miami and Erie Canal, this beautiful park offers hiking trails along the old towpath, picnic facilities, and camping (no electricity, vault toilets). Three miles of riverside riding are available in the park, and a historical marker at the entrance to the park provides information about the old canal.

2. **Route Note**
   Travelers are reminded to use extra caution when traveling along or crossing state routes, such as SR 24.

3. **1899 Schoolhouse**
   Like all the old schoolhouses along the loop, this one room brick schoolhouse is located on private property but is clearly in view from the road.

4. **St. Markus Kirche**
   This beautiful brick country church, built by the descendants of the German pioneer families in the area, dates back to 1895.

5. **1894 Schoolhouse**

6. **Goll Woods State Nature Preserve**
   Visitors to this beautiful primeval woodland are reminded to "take only photographs and leave only footprints". Trails are available, as is parking and restroom facilities. The entrance is located along TR 26.

7. **Goll Cemetery**
   Located just west of the loop on TR F is the historic Goll Cemetery, where the generations of the Golls are buried. It is due to their foresightedness that we are able to enjoy this last remaining remnant of the great Ohio forest in this part of the state.

8. **1883 Schoolhouse**

9. **1876 Schoolhouse**

10. **Route Note**
    There is a one-quarter mile stretch of gravel road between SR 34 and SR 66.

11. **Bethlehem Lutheran Church**
    Located along the curve in Adams Ridge Rd. is this charming brick country church. The date plate, however, is broken and illegible.

12. **Cemetery**
    This little cemetery is unusual due to the arrangement of stones in a semi-circle at the rear of the cemetery.

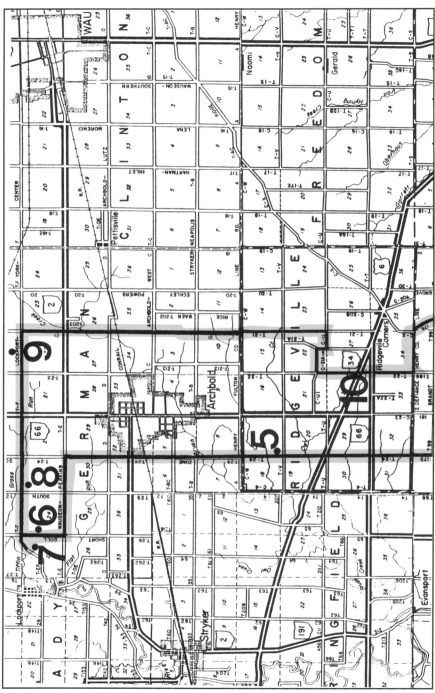

LOOP #29
Northern Half

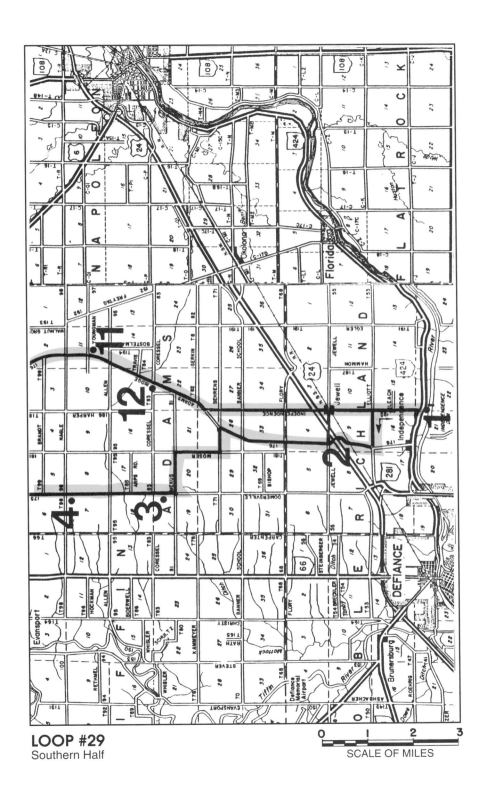

LOOP #29
Southern Half

SCALE OF MILES

0   1   2   3

LOOP #30

Length: 47/31 miles

Terrain: Flat to rolling

County: Fulton/Williams

The Great Northwest Tour

This enchanting tour through the northwest corner of Ohio takes the traveler from Harrison Lake State Park through the countryside of Williams County, stretching over the gently rolling terrain to visit prehistoric Indian mounds in Ohio's most northwesterly township. Along the way are century old country churches and peaceful pioneer cemeteries, nestled in valleys that are home to beautiful barns and rolling green pastures, lakes that offer rest to wildlife and wanderer alike, and a historic log cabin that sits on a hill looking over the fertile fields around it.

Traveling through an area of open countryside, it's easy to imagine that what we see is all there ever was, with the exception of perhaps a few trees. But the land is like a chalkboard, having been written upon and erased, time after time. Empty crossroads may have been towns, and fields of corn may grow over old battlefields. Only rarely does the eraser of time miss its mark, and leave a covered bridge, an old mill, a one-room schoolhouse, or perhaps a log cabin, protruding above the sands of time for even a century. How extraordinary it is indeed when a signpost of a civilization that thrived here 2,000 years ago remains for today's explorer to visit, casting the imagination back to that long ago time.

Two millenia ago, an elaborate and artistic society was centered in the Ohio Valley, a society that we today call the Hopewell. Living chiefly in riverside towns, the people of this society built great burial mounds and earthworks, and carried on trading from the Rockies to the Atlantic. The mounds left behind by this vanished society were cause for great, and often wild, speculation by the first settlers who came into Ohio. The Indians living here at the time were equally puzzled as to who built the mysterious mounds. It is unusual to find the remnants of the Hopewell Culture this far north in Ohio, but the four inauspicious mounds of earth along Nettle Creek in Williams County give testimony that the Hopewells were indeed here.

After visiting the mounds at Nettle Creek, a rest awaits you at beautiful Lake La Su An before you journey on through Pioneer, Ohio and back to Harrison Lake for a refreshing swim at journey's end. For persons wishing not to travel so far back in time, a short cut is provided on the map after your visit to the restored log cabin and metal bridge.

POINTS OF INTEREST:

1. **Harrison Lake State Park**
   Class A (electricity and showers) and B (no electric, latrines) camping is available at this state park, as well as swimming and picnicking.

2. **1875 Church**

3. **Jacob Young Log House**

4. **1909 Metal Bridge**

5. **Church Bell and Old Millstone**
   Located at SR 576 and P-50, the 1892 bell sits in front of the old church. On the same corner is an old millstone with a historical marker indicating that the stone was first used in a mill built in 1844, and later used in a mill in 1852 that was located one-half mile east of this spot.

6. **Nettle Lake Indian Mounds**
   The drive that leads back to the mounds is easy to miss, especially when the corn is up. It is located precisely one-half mile north of road R on the east side of road 4.75. Historical markers describe the history of the mounds and the Hopewells.

7. **Nettle Lake U.B. Church and Cemetery**
   Veterans of the Civil War and the War of 1812 are buried in this peaceful little cemetery across from the old church, which was struck by the 1991 tornado.

8. **Lake La Su An**
   This beautiful wildlife area is operated by the Ohio Department of Natural Resources as a hunting and fishing preserve.

9. **North Bridgewater Church**
   Located at SR 576 and R, this picturesque church is more ornate than many of its type.

10. **Pioneer, Ohio**
    As you pass through the center of this quaint village, you will make a slight left jog at the traffic light.

A Note to the Navigator: Williams County uses a simple grid system in numbering their roads. East-west roads are lettered, south-north roads are numbered, consecutively, at one mile intervals. Roads located between the intervals use decimals, e.g. P-50 is an east-west road halfway between P and Q; 4.75 is a north-south road located three-fourths of the way between roads 4 and 5. Because the county has chosen to use two different systems for their maps and road signage, a grid has been added as a key for identifying all roads in the county. Each road along this loop is identified in parentheses at each turn. Simply use the parentheses and the grid in identifying the roads in Williams County.

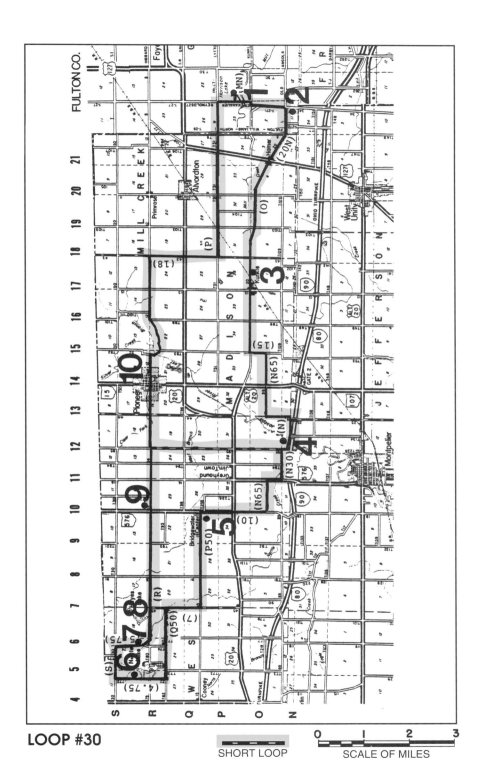

LOOP #30

SHORT LOOP

SCALE OF MILES

0   1   2   3

LOOP #31

Length: 14 miles

Terrain: Flat to gently rolling

County: Ottawa/Erie

Island of Stone

Islands and intrigue seem to go hand in hand, and this sojourn to a place apart can only be described as enchanting. You will tour along the rocky shores of the largest American island in Lake Erie, looking out over the sparkling blue waters, the music of the waves accompanying you as you pedal past Ice Age wonders, Indian mysteries, and the magnificent stone mansions of Kelleys Island.

The story of Kelleys Island is literally written in the rocks, and our island explorer will be able to trace 25,000 years of history in the beautiful limestone of the island. The earliest chapter of the story was written during the Ice Age by the awesome power of a glacier. Far to the north in Canada, snow and ice began piling up, ultimately reaching a height of 8,000 feet. Like putty, the weight of this mass forced the edge to begin spreading out, and as it crept across the landscape, it filled in valleys and rounded off hilltops. On Kelleys Island, the power and artistry of the glacier can be seen in the 400 foot long grooves scoured into the limestone as the glacier's icy edge passed. The world famous Glacial Grooves of Kelleys Island have been a wonder to visitors for over a century.

Mother Nature is not the only writer in rock to have left a legacy on the island. More than three hundred years ago, the Erie Indians, or People of the Panther, lived here. In 1655, a fierce and feared confederation called the Five Nations swept through here like a terrible storm, vanquishing and eliminating the Cat Nation. All that remains of these people on the island today are mysterious, and nearly obliterated, pictographs carved into the smooth surface of Inscription Rock, a large boulder that juts into the water on the south side of the island.

While the glacier and the Indians carved their stories into the rocks, another island author wrote his story with the rocks themselves. Nicholas Smith emigrated from Bavaria in 1858, coming to

Kelleys Island around 1860. Smith was a stone mason, and when this skilled artisan took the beautiful and prized Kelleys Island limestone in hand, the results were many of the beautiful stone buildings that dot the island and delight passersby. Mr. Smith continued to work with stone until he was 80 years old, when he turned to grape growing. Century old stone churches, schools, wine cellars and houses are the monuments to the stone mason's craft standing yet today on Kelleys Island.

With the glacial grooves, Inscription Rock, quarries and beautiful buildings, a trip to Kelleys Island is a trip to a fascinating gallery of stone.

POINTS OF INTEREST:

1. *Neuman Ferry Dock, Marblehead, Ohio*
   This island adventure begins with a 30 minute ferry ride to the island from the dock at the foot of Francis St. in Marblehead. The cost is about $10.00 round trip for an adult with a bicycle. Contact the carrier at (419) 626-5557 to confirm the schedule and prices. Frequent trips.

2. *Ferry Dock, Kelleys Island*
   To begin your explorations, turn left after leaving the dock.

3. *Sunset Point*
   This is a favored vantage point for the fabled Kelleys sunsets.

4. *Limestone Quarries*
   On the east side of the road are the old stone quarries. Limestone for the first American lock at the Soo was quarried from Kelleys Island, as were the stone border markers for the Indiana-Ohio state line.

5. *Glacial Grooves*
   Considered the most spectacular glacial grooves in the world, this famous site is now under the auspices of the Ohio Historical Society.

6. *Kelleys Island State Park*
   A public beach and camping facilities are available at this state park.

7. *Kelleys Island Cemetery*
   In the north end of the cemetery are buried the island's pro-prietor, Datus Kelley, and his family, including Charles Carpenter, son-in-law and the island's first vintner, and Addison, Datus' son

and first resident of the Kelley Mansion. Local legend has it that John McDonald was working on preparing the cemetery, and when accused of poor work habits, replied that he would not ever be buried in the cemetery, so he didn't care. Shortly afterwards, he met an untimely end in the quarry where he worked, and in 1854, became the very first person buried in the cemetery. His grave is in the far northwest corner.

8. *Estes School*
   Built in 1901 using funds given by James Estes, the school is now famous for its one-member graduating classes.

9. *North Bay Scenic Spur*
   This dead-end road follows the scenic rocky shore of the island's North Bay.

10. *1865 Home of Nicholas Smith*
    This was the home of Nicholas Smith, the stone mason, and his wife. It is now the tasting room of the resurrected Kelleys Island Wine Co.

11. *Kelley Mansion*
    Built for Addison Kelley during the Civil War years of 1861-65, the mansion is on the National Register of Historic Places. Presidents Taft and McKinley have stayed here. The most famous feature of the mansion is the circular staircase in the main hall, built from a single piece of wood. The mansion is open daily for tours. Admission fee.

12. *Inscription Rock*
    Henry Schoolcraft, historian and Indian agent, said of Inscription Rock in the early 19th century, "It is by far the most extensive and well sculptured and best preserved inscription of the antiquarian period ever found in America." The rock has suffered the elements, and is now nearly obliterated. It is a site of the Ohio Historical Society.

13. *South Shore Scenic Spur*
    Civil War era stone houses look out over the blue waters along this scenic spur. Turning around is advised where the road turns north and becomes gravel.

14. *Kelley Hall*

This Town Hall was a gift to the community from Datus Kelley in 1860. It has seen a variety of uses, ranging from the first high school to church services to a library.

15. *South Side School*

Located in the "downtown" section of the island on the west side of Division Street, this 1853 stone school building is now a rooming house.

16. *Old Stone Church*

This picturesque stone church was built by the German speaking German Reformed Church in 1867. Its last service was the burial of a life-long member in 1942. It is now home to the Kelleys Island Historical Association.

17. *Winery Ruins*

Barely visible through the foliage, the castle-like ruins of the old winery are on private property. The wine industry of Kelleys Island began in the mid-1850's, and of the sparkling Catawba wine it was said that "having once tasted for medicinal purposes only, a Rechabite in temperance in a season of despondency would be sorely tempted for a revivification merely to yield his willing lips".

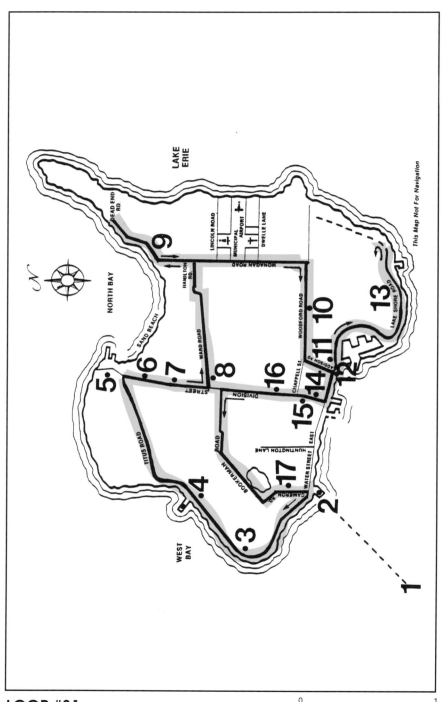

LOOP #31

0   1

LOOP #32

Length: 45 miles

Terrain: Gently rolling

County: Mercer

The Road to Recovery

This 45 mile tour over the gently rolling terrain of Mercer County will take you past the fields and meadows of the dairy farms that form the agricultural patchwork of this region. Bovines grazing on the slopes beneath the spires of the tall country churches create a pastoral scene where you will find abandoned one-room schoolhouses, metal bridges, old cemeteries, and one of the most sacred memorials to the men who first ventured into the wilderness of the Ohio Country.

It was just before sunrise on the snowy morning of November 4, 1791. Sent by President Washington to still the Indian attacks along the frontier, the army of General Arthur St. Clair had encamped on the banks of the Wabash River. Suddenly, out of the stillness of early morning came the war whoops of the Indian forces led by Blue Jacket, Little Turtle, and Simon Girty. The unprepared soldiers were completely overwhelmed, and 631 men gave their lives that day. Two years later, General Anthony Wayne, called by the Indians the "American general who never sleeps", returned to the site of the defeat and built Fort Recovery. On June 30, 1794, one of the largest Indian forces ever to engage the American Army attacked the fort. On the site of previous disaster, the forces of General Wayne prevailed, delivering a defeat to the Indians that broke their spirit. Two months later, the war was over with Wayne's victory at Fallen Timbers. So important were these events at Fort Recovery that the Congress erected a memorial that stands today on the square in Fort Recovery, Ohio. The 93 foot high granite shaft entombs the fallen heroes "who, as advance guards, entered the wilderness of the west to blaze the way for freedom and civilization".

After visiting the memorial and the partially reconstructed fort, you'll follow the Greenville Treaty Line out of town and into the beautiful countryside of "The Land of the Cross-Tipped

Churches". Picturesque churches dating back nearly a century, tall steeples reaching to the skies, ring the horizon as you ride slowly through this scenic panorama of western Ohio. The names of the small towns and roads along the route bear witness to the importance of the church to these rural communities, names such as St. Rose, St. Wendelin, St. Sebastian, St. Henry, and many more. Biblical names abound on the maps and road signs. The close reader of the map will notice that even the county map maker got caught up in the spirit by identifying our road toward Minster as "Fort Recovery-Minister" Rd.

POINTS OF INTEREST:

1. *Grand Lake St. Mary's*
   The ride begins at the western end of the lake at the picnic grounds, just south of the east terminus of Monroe Road. Grand Lake, built to feed the canal system, was dug from a swamp by 1,700 men who worked for $0.30 a day plus a jigger of whiskey. At the time it was completed, it was the largest man-made lake in the world.

2. *Route Note*
   Bicyclists depart from the roadway to take the Celina-Coldwater Bikeway to Coldwater. At the end of the bikeway in Coldwater, turn right on Vine to SR 118, then south through town. Motorists may follow the marked roads on the map to reach Coldwater.

3. *St. Peter Church*
   Built in 1904, this is but one of the many cross-tipped churches that loom over the landscape of Mercer County.

4. *Route Note*
   Turn south onto First St. from Wabash Rd. just inside the Fort Recovery city limit, crossing over the Wabash River.

5. *Fort Recovery Memorial*
   Located at First St. and Boundary in the town square, this monument was erected in 1912 by Act of Congress.

6. *Fort Recovery Historical Site and Museum*
Two reconstructed blockhouses and a connecting stockade are found at this Ohio Historical Society site. The museum located here is open June through August, Tues.-Sat. 1-5, Sun. 12-5; weekends in May and September. Admission charge for museum. The site is located west of the square on Boundary St.

7. *Greenville Treaty Line*
Following Anthony Wayne's victory at Fallen Timbers, the Treaty of Greene Ville was signed in 1795. The Indians conceded land south of the line to settlement, while retaining use of land to the north of the line. Boundary Road follows the line east out of town, where it becomes Ft. Recovery-Minster Rd.

8. *One Room Schoolhouse*
This quaint one room schoolhouse, long out of service and on private property, was built in 1900.

9. *St. Wendelin Church*

10. *1905 St. Francisci Church*

11. *Steepleview Stretch*
This stretch of Homan Road is noted for the number of steeples that can be seen from this vantage point.

12. *St. Sebastian Church*

13. *Route Note: Caution*
Use extra caution along this half-mile stretch of U.S. 127. The road is very busy, but there is a berm available.

14. *The Big Chicken*
In front of the Heyne's egg farm stands the Big Chicken, and an interesting painting on the barn portrays another chicken. The farm even has drive-thru egg pickup.

15. *Route Note*
Cyclists can again pick up the bikeway on St. Anthony Road. Motorists can follow the map back to the picnic grounds at Grand Lake St. Marys.

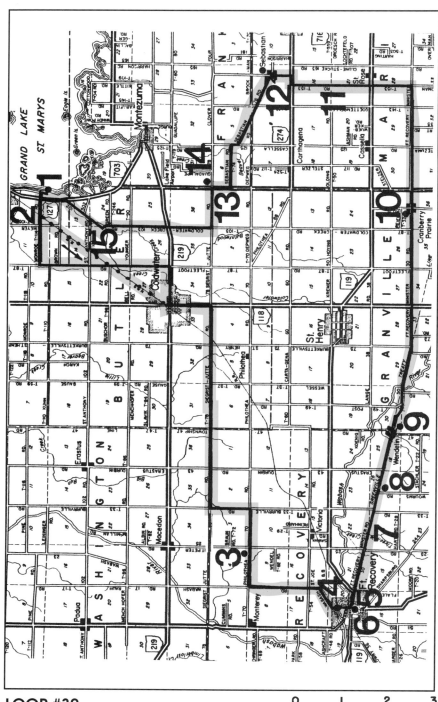

LOOP #32

0   1   2   3

SCALE OF MILES

LOOP #33

Length: 21 miles

Terrain: Flat to gently rolling

County: Auglaize

Top of the Canal

This 21 mile tour from Grand Lake St. Mary's takes the twentieth century traveler back more than one-hundred years to the days of the Miami and Erie Canal, the days of mules, mills, towpaths, and boom towns. Beginning at Grand Lake, which was the world's largest man-made reservoir and fed the canal, we travel south through two canal era towns, one still thriving, the other just surviving, past remnants of those romantic days, the brick canal houses and old locks. One-room schoolhouses from the turn of the century stand along the loop, and a stop at the ponds of the state's fish farm rounds out this ride through beautiful Auglaize County.

The flat to gently rolling terrain of western Auglaize County belies the fact that as you travel through this area, you are crossing a "great divide" known as the Loramie Summit, the highest point on the Miami and Erie Canal. This summit was 21 miles long, a plateau of water that was held in place by two locks, designated Number One South at Lockington and Number One North at New Bremen. From New Bremen, canal boats on the way to Cincinnati "locked down" 513 feet in vertical distance to the Ohio River; boats on the way to Toledo locked down 395 feet to Lake Erie. The north lock can be seen holding back water yet today in New Bremen, and a number of canal era buildings still stand near the old canal, giving us a glimpse of that by-gone era.

From Lock One we head north along the banks of the old canal through the village of Lock Two, Ohio. The prosperity and growth that characterized New Bremen gave promise to Lock Two as well, and the canal gave rise to a three story mill that stands at the Village Commons. The early miller's residence, now a private home, stands across from the mill, and the barn on the right as you enter the town served as a warehouse during the canal era. The large brick home and the old store across the

Commons likewise date back to the canal days, being owned by John Garmhausen, who came to America from Germany in 1836. After seeking his fortune in California during the Gold Rush days, it seems that he "struck gold" here in Ohio along the waters of the old canal. As the canal waters vanished with the coming of the railroad, so did the prosperity of many of the towns that had sprung up along the "Big Ditch". Today, the mill is boarded up, and business life is virtually gone from Lock Two. Yet, it takes only a little imagination to look over to the banks and see the mules plodding along the towpaths, and to hear the rushing of the water as Lock Two empties and fills, a sound that transforms, if only in the mind, a ghost-like town back into the bustling canal town of a century ago.

Campers are advised that another day of exploring is available with the "Fort Amanda Tour", which also departs from Grand Lake St. Mary's State Park.

POINTS OF INTEREST:

1. *Grand Lake St. Mary's State Park*
   The tour begins at the East Embankment picnic area at the east end of the lake just south of the railroad tracks. Cyclists may want to follow the park road south along the shore of the lake, then cut over to SR 364 at the end of the park road. To reach the park's camping and swimming areas, enter off of nearby SR 364/703 west.

2. *Feeder Canal*
   After your turn onto CR 114A, you will ride alongside the old feeder canal that carried water from the reservoir into the canal system. American water lilies now blossom in the canal.

3. *One-Room Schoolhouse*
   This ornate old brick schoolhouse, long out of service, stands on private property at the terminus of Waesch Rd.

4. *1902 Schoolhouse*
   At the top of a gentle rise stands this early one-room schoolhouse, its bell tower, complete with bell, silhouetted against the sky. School days are over for this beautiful building, and it has been converted into a private residence.

5. *New Bremen, Ohio*

Follow the "local truck route" signs through the streets of this charming village, past the museum and other early brick homes. Turn left at SR 274 (Monroe St.) to pass through the quaint business section on your way to the canal lock, which is located on the south side of Monroe St. at Washington Street. In front of the library on S. Washington is the historical marker describing the lock. Leaving town by going north on Jefferson St. (New Bremen-New Knoxville Rd.) from Monroe St., you will pass by a canal house built in 1853 that faces the old canal. The museum on N. Main is open Sundays June-Aug., 2-4.

6. *Lock Two, Ohio*

7. *Route Note*

Use extra caution on this short stretch of SR 66. A berm is available for cyclists.

8. *St. Mary's Fish Farm*

Fifty-two acres of ponds are located here at the state's fish farm, where pike, bass, and other fish are raised. As you ride slowly along the dikes between the ponds, you will observe many waterfowl and shore birds, especially during the seasonal migrations of spring and fall. Visiting hours are 9 to 4.

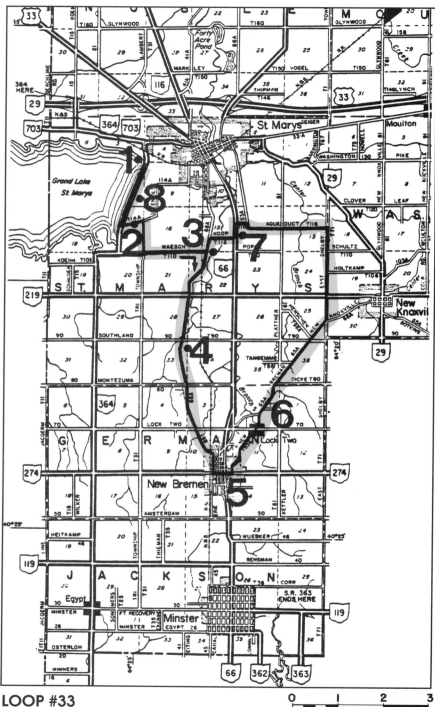

LOOP #33

SCALE OF MILES

0   1   2   3

LOOP #34

Length: 42 miles

Terrain: Flat to gently rolling

County: Auglaize

The Fort Amanda Tour

This 42 mile tour through northwest Auglaize County winds along quiet country roads, past peaceful ponds and over old metal bridges on the way to the site of Fort Amanda, which played an important role in the War of 1812. Along the way are one room schoolhouses, brick country churches, and vestiges of the old Miami and Erie Canal, including one canal feature so spectacular it is on the National Register of Historic Places.

It has been said that cemeteries are history books of stone, and our visit to the site of Fort Amanda brings to life an important chapter in Ohio's turbulent past. Northwest Ohio had been a battleground during the 1790's, as three American generals had tried to defeat the Indians and open the area for settlement. It took only eight years from Anthony Wayne's victory at Fallen Timbers for Ohio to become the 17th state, and after only nine years of statehood, Ohio again became a battleground. The War of 1812 in Ohio was a war waged not only against the British, but against the Indians of Tecumseh's Federation as well. Fort Amanda was constructed by General William Henry Harrison in 1812 to protect the supply lines that reached north to the Maumee Rapids, and the fort also served as a hospital for wounded soldiers returning from the front.

Today, the site of the old fort is marked by a 50 foot high obelisk, and the path leading to the memorial takes us past the 1814 U.S. Cemetery where 75 soldiers who died at the fort are buried. When the British burned the War Records Office in Washington, D.C. in 1814, the identities of these countrymen were forever lost. The white military markers of these Unknown Soldiers read simply, "U.S. Soldier, War of 1812". Another marker testifying to the Indian aspect of the war is inscribed "Capt. E. Dawson, Murdered by Indians, Oct. 1812", and an earlier veteran from the Revolutionary War, William Taylor of the New Jersey Militia, is also buried here.

143

Heroic deeds are, of course, not limited to war and strife. The traveler along this route will pass by an epic feat of another kind, a feature simply called "Deep Cut". Carved by hand through the dirt and rock, this 6,600 foot long cut on the Miami and Erie Canal is one of the most spectacular hand-excavated canal projects ever undertaken, and has earned a place in the National Register of Historic Places. Today, Deep Cut serves as a memorial to the industriousness and perseverance of the early builders of Ohio.

Campers are advised that another day of exploring is available with the "Top of the Canal Tour", also departing from Grand Lake St. Marys.

POINTS OF INTEREST:

1. *Grand Lake St. Marys State Park*
   The tour begins at this state park, where camping, swimming, and picnicking are available. Use extra caution on the road leading from the park.

2. *Metal Bridge*

3. *Forty Acre Pond*
   Travelers seeking a quiet spot for reflection will enjoy passing by this serene pond, a wide water of the old canal.

4. *Metal Bridge*

5. *Route Note*
   Cyclists are advised to use extra caution when traveling along or crossing state routes such as SR 197, 66, and 198.

6. *Miami and Erie Canal*
   You will be traveling along a water-filled section of the Miami and Erie Canal as you head north along CR 66A.

7. *Deep Cut*
   The Cut is visible from the little bridge on Deep Cut Road over the canal, and a roadside park on the west side of SR 66 provides another view of the canal and towpath here.

8. **1885 Schoolhouse**

For the hard working German immigrants of the late 19th century, this was the place many of them first learned to speak the language of their new country. The land on which the school stands was once purchased by a Mr. Fischer for a pair of leather boots. It is now private property.

9. **Fort Amanda Historical Site**

Operated by The Ohio Historical Society, the site is open daily. Picnic tables are located at the site.

10. **Glynwood, Ohio**

An 1883 brick country church and an 1899 one room schoolhouse stand at the intersection in the crossroads town of Glynwood.

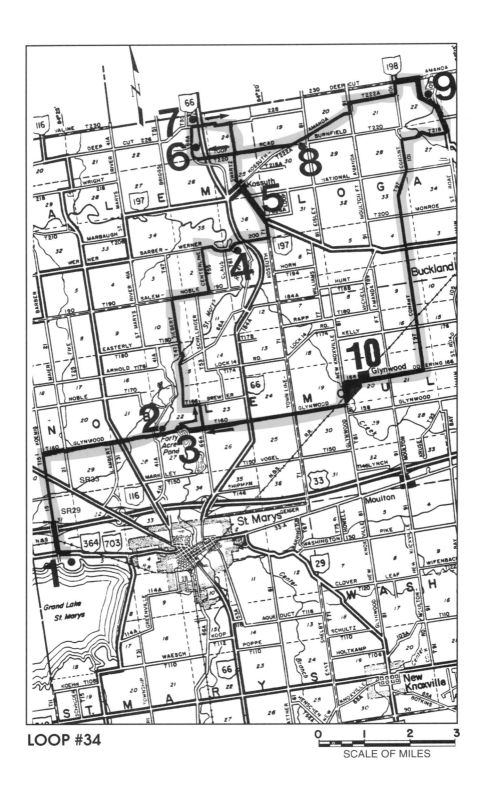

LOOP #34

0   1   2   3
SCALE OF MILES

LOOP #35

Length: 31 miles

Terrain: Flat

County: Wood

Red Barn Country

This 31 mile ramble through the countryside of Wood County meanders along the banks of the beautiful Portage River before passing through an early metal bridge that serves as a gateway to the fields and farms of this red barn country. Egrets and herons can be seen standing in the riffles of the river, and golden rolls of hay dot the summertime fields along these country roads. In addition to simply enjoying this pastoral scene, the traveler along this loop can visit the grave of one of the famous Andrews Raiders of Civil War fame and tour the Old Infirmary, built well over a century ago as the county's "poor house". Now the home of the Wood County museum, exhibits of nineteenth century living, ranging from the macabre to the quaint, are housed in the old institution.

There are few scenes more enchanting to the backroad explorer than those featuring big red barns and golden fields. Perhaps it is because our national heritage is rooted on the farm that we have a sense of coming home when we travel these narrow country lanes, passing by the old homesteads, clothes hanging on the line and a tire swing dangling from a tree. Although life on the farm today is far from idyllic, and involves seemingly unending work, something was added to the land-scape here a little more than 50 years ago that changed life on the farm in a dramatic fashion. Now taken for granted and little noticed by the passerby, the coming of the wooden utility poles was eagerly watched and anticipated by the farm families of the 1930's. Because running lines to the isolated farms was not cost efficient for the power companies of the day, farmers formed co-ops, and with the assistance of the federal govern-ment, began setting the poles and stringing the lines that brought an end to much of the drudgery of farm work.

The day the lights came on in the country was not a day without problems, however. Like anything else, it took some

getting used to. According to the Ohio Rural Electric Coopera-
tives, one woman used a pot holder to turn on her light switches,
while another kept her outlets plugged to keep the electricity
from draining out. The Rural Electric Administration received a
letter from another woman who, although quite pleased with the
electricity, had trouble sleeping with the light on in her bedroom.
She was instructed in how to operate the switch on the wall. And
what was the most desired appliance after electricity came? The
electric washing machine topped the list.

Finally, the traveler along the loop will see barns of various
sizes and shapes, including the beautiful bank barn, named for
the dirt bank that leads up to the second floor. Animals entered
their quarters on the first floor on the side opposite the bank in
such barns. Bank barns originated in the mountainous country of
Pennsylvania, but were so efficient that they were adopted even
in the flatlands. Roof styles also vary from barn to barn, and the
"bent-roof" design seen on many barns in rural Ohio is called
"gambrel". Following a visit to the Old Infirmary, the sharp-eyed
scout will spot a beautiful barn combining the gambrel roof and
bank design standing along the loop.

With the magnificent barns, scenic river, old bridges, and,
yes, even wooden utility poles, this ride through the countryside is
truly a tonic for the harried.

POINTS OF INTEREST:

1. **William Henry Harrison Park**
   The loop begins at this county park located on Pemberville
   Road (Bierley Rd.) at the southern boundary of Pemberville.
   Picnic tables, restrooms, and drinking water are available here,
   and the park is open daily.

2. **Route Note**
   Be cautious as you cross busy SR 6.

3. **1898 Metal Bridge**
   Built by the Canton Bridge Builders nearly a century ago, this old
   bridge spans the Portage River.

4. **Route Note**
   Pass straight through this intersection both times, making this a
   "figure-eight" loop.

148

5. The Old Infirmary

Home to the Wood County Historical Society, the museum is open Apr.-Oct. for tours Thur., Fri. and Sunday 1-3. There is an admission charge.

6. Paupers Cemetery

A lone marker stands by the road south of the Old Infirmary, marking the old paupers cemetery. All the other markers, which bore only a number and no name, were removed from here in the 1950's.

7. Route Note

County Home Road makes a right jog over the freeway at Kramer Road.

8. Grave of Elihu Mason

A marker stands at the main Pemberville Cemetery entrance, describing the feats of Mason and his fellow Raiders. His gray obelisk marker is located just a few stones southwest of the center crossroads in the cemetery. The crossroads are marked by a single tree standing at the juncture. (See loop #26 for Andrews Raiders information.)

9. Pemberville, Ohio

After entering the town, turn right on Bridge Street at the 1902 Township Hall, then right on Bierley Rd. to return to the park.

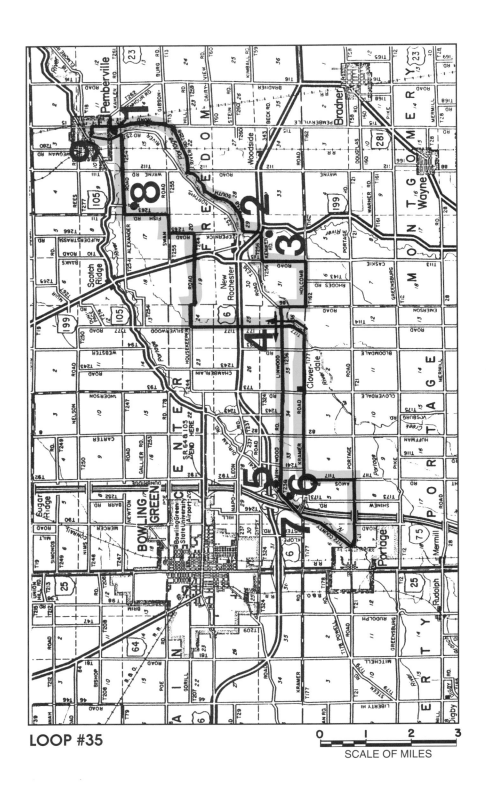

LOOP #35

0 1 2 3

SCALE OF MILES

SECTION IV. *Northeast Ohio*

Doyle Road Covered Bridge. Loop #42

Trip Planning Guide
Northeast Ohio

# Name	Length short (miles) loop	Historical site	Nature preserve	Museum	Covered bridge(s)	Pioneer cemetery	Picnic area	Camping (state/county park)	Swimming	Walking trails
36. Milan Miles	42	X		X			X			
37. Heartland Ramble	43 (32)	X				X				
38. New Connecticut, Old Order	50		X				X		X	X
39. Malabar Farm	41	X	X	X		X	X	X		X
40. Pasture Primer	30	X		X		X	X			X
41. The Ohio & Erie Canal	17	X		X	X	X	X			X
42. Covered Bridge Country	48				X					

Tour Loop Locations
Northeast Ohio

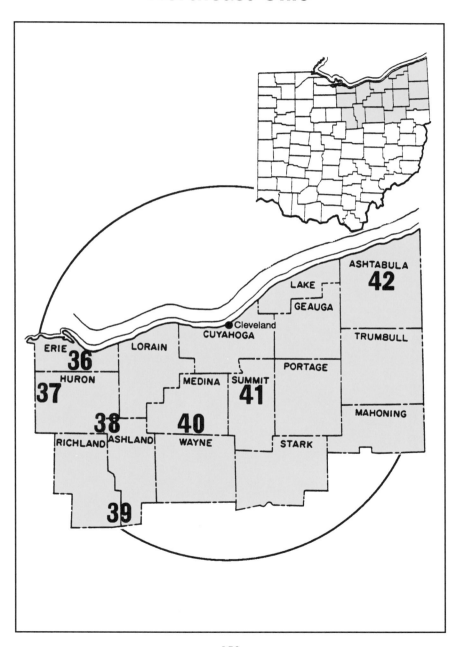

LOOP #36

Length: 42 miles

Terrain: Flat to gently rolling, with some hills by rivers

County: Erie/Huron

Milan Miles

This loop, just inland from the south shore of Lake Erie, begins in the charming New England-like village that produced America's greatest inventor, then winds past old churches, canal remnants, and beautiful stone houses on the way to a restored historic village and one of the oldest churches in the Firelands. Tranquil countryside and beautiful river valleys grace the landscape of this Erie County meander, where the mind of a young boy named Thomas Edison was being shaped a century and a half ago.

Who can say what gives rise to genius? If it is the meeting of a fertile mind with a stimulating environment, Milan and young Tom Edison were well matched. It was here in 1847, the year of Edison's birth, that one could see lake schooners tied up at the loading docks, taking on their shipments of wheat and other produce. It was a time of innovation and industry, and Milan was booming. Her canal had just been completed, and it was not just a barge canal like the other Ohio canals, it was a ship's canal, where the sailing vessels of Lake Erie could sail down the Huron River to the canal and into town. Ships were being built, hundreds of grain wagons unloaded, and colorful canal characters roamed the streets and square. Imagine the excitement and stimulation it offered the young boy who lived up on the hill in the brick house overlooking the canal basin in those heady years of the mid-nineteenth century. Perhaps that boy would have gone on to greatness in another environment, or perhaps it was the excitement and stimulation this little village offered that made the difference. But in any case, Milan produced along the banks of the old canal a boy who was to become one of the greatest inventors in the history of the world.

The time that the boy Edison and Milan shared was brief, for the days of the canal were numbered. When the railroad usurped the business of the canal, the town lost much of her population, including the Edisons, who all left except for one of Thomas's sisters, who had just married Homer Page and set up housekeeping on a nearby farm. Although Thomas and his family left Milan when he was only seven years old, it was this town that he remembered as home, and it was to this place that he brought his good friends in later life, Henry Ford and Harvey Firestone, to travel these country roads and gaze again at familiar landmarks. He even bought back the house on the hill where he was born. The saying "no man is a prophet in his own land" must have gone through Edison's mind when he visited his birthplace in 1923, for it was still lit by candlelight decades after he invented the incandescent light bulb. Travelers today along this loop will follow roads out of Milan and into the township that Ford, Firestone, and Edison almost certainly traveled more than half a century ago, when the inventor returned for the final time to his "beloved hills of Milan".

Leaving Milan Township, the route meanders westward toward Historic Lyme Village and its neighbor, one of the earliest churches in the Firelands, the Lyme Congregational Church. Revealing its New England heritage through its architecture, the sanctuary of the old church is on the second floor. Their Sunday School was the fourth one started in Ohio, and with the subsequent closing of the others, this Sunday School has the distinction of being the oldest in the state. Funds for the church, built in 1835-36, were raised through the sale of pews, which netted from $20 to $125 at auction. Of course, the more expensive seats were at the back of the church, a trend which would probably continue to this day. Following your visit to the old church and the village, you'll wind your way back to Milan through beautiful countryside, crossing the scenic valley of the Huron River with its brooding cliffs of shale, before climbing the hills back to the loop's beginning.

POINTS OF INTEREST:

1. *Milan, Ohio*
   Beautiful homes of Greek Revival architecture, reminiscent of New England, grace the streets of this charming village. Edison's birthplace, on N. Edison St., is open for tours (admission charge, closed Dec.-Jan., and winter Mondays). The only surviving warehouse from the canal days is at the bottom of the hill from N. Main St. beside the railroad tracks that run through the old

basin. Metal bridge buffs will be interested in the stone abutments where the now closed road would have crossed the Huron River, for these abutments supported the first iron bridge built by Milan's Zenas King, who went on to become a millionaire bridge builder. The bridge collapsed into the river in 1935 when struck by a truck.

2. *Milan Cemetery*
From Edison's birthplace, the loop goes south on Edison St., then left on Berlin St. After your turn onto Berlin, you will see a striking family mausoleum with the name Fries upon it located by the road in Milan Cemetery. Valentine Fries was a wealthy shipbuilder here in the nineteenth century, with three dozen ships sailing the lakes. The tomb is considered one of the best examples of Tunic architecture in the country, and was dedicated by his wife in 1906.

3. *Camp Avery Historical Marker*
This marker stands near the site of Camp Avery, a fortification built in 1811 to protect the settlers from Indians and British on the eve of the War of 1812. Gravestones of a Revolutionary War veteran and a War of 1812 veteran are also found by the marker.

4. *Milan Canal Towpath*
The canal towpath, one of the few remnants of the three mile long Milan Canal, can be seen paralleling the railroad tracks south of Mason Rd.

5. *Homer Page Farm*
The big red barn you see on the rise after crossing the Huron River is on the Homer Page Farm. Thomas Edison's sister married Homer Page around 1849, and the farm is still in the Edison family today.

6. *1897 Friends Church*

7. *Merry Schoolhouse Site*
The schoolhouse has been moved to Historic Lyme Village.

8. *1866 St. John's Evangelical Church*

9. *Route Note*
Use extra caution along this stretch of road due to truck traffic.

10. *Parkertown Restaurant*
While the restaurant may be modest, their pride in Parkertown, now a crossroads huddled beneath an overpass, runs deep. Fascinating old photos and other memorabilia hang on the walls, and the cane of Mr. Parker, the town's founder, is displayed proudly on the wall. The number of trucks parked here testifies to the good home cooking.

11. *Route Note*
Use extra caution on this stretch of State Route 4.

12. *Lyme Church*

13. *Historic Lyme Village*
This historic village, with the magnificent Wright Mansion as the centerpiece, is home to a number of early buildings that have been relocated here. Old log houses, a blacksmith shop, and the National Museum of the Postmark Collectors Club are some of the attractions found in the village. Open daily except Monday, 1 to 5, June through August; only on Sundays in May and September. Admission charge.

14. *Stone House Stretch*
Several early stone houses of beautiful limestone can be seen as you travel this section of Strecker Road.

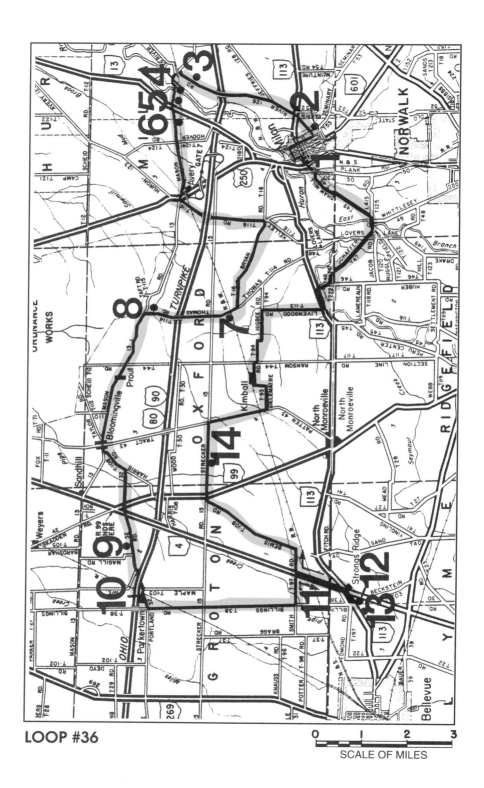

LOOP #36

SCALE OF MILES

0   1   2   3

LOOP #37

Length: 43/32 miles

Terrain: Flat to gently rolling

County: Huron/Seneca

Heartland Ramble

Ohio has been called the heart of the nation, and Huron County might well be considered the heart of Ohio. This beautiful farmland in north-central Ohio is home to country churches, one-room schoolhouses, old metal bridges, pioneer cemeteries, beautiful farms and farmhouses. Strawberry fields of spring yielding to the corn and wheat fields of summer mark the passage of time over the gently rolling landscape of this rich agricultural area. Add to this tapestry an old stagecoach inn and the last remnant of a rural ghost town, and a day of backroad exploring is at hand.

The traveler along this loop in midsummer will see huge combines, silhouetted against a blue sky, combing golden fields of wheat. Wheat helped put this area on the agricultural map as far back as 1839, when the Milan Canal opened on the Huron River. So productive were these lands that Milan was second only to Odessa, Russia in the amount of wheat passing through her port, and this rich harvest supported more than just the farmer. Hundreds of huge grain wagons, known as "land schooners", rumbled over these roads on their way to the wharves, and the men who drove the wagons needed a place to stay at night. Because roads were notoriously poor and overland travel painfully slow, the roadside tavern filled a pressing need.

Evenings at these inns were often boisterous times, with stagecoach drivers, teamsters, and travelers congregating to drink and swap stories. Colorful characters and even more colorful language were hallmarks of the old inns. With all the activity, the tavern became a magnet for the isolated people in the countryside, who were drawn to the taprooms for entertainment and news from the outside world. Daniel Mack's stagecoach inn at Macksville, now a crossroads hamlet known as Peru, was one such stop. It was not unusual for 25 teams and teamsters to put up here, and the going rate for a man and four horses was about fifty cents a night. The teams and teamsters are gone, but the old Macksville Tavern stands yet today by a free-flowing spring that attracts people from the countryside thirsty for water and news.

At the same time business at the Macksville Tavern was booming, the Second Regular Baptist Church was being built at Omar. According to *The Ohio Ghost Town Gazette*, it was to serve "as a meeting house for a place of worship, but not to be at any time used by themselves nor let out to others so as that any password shall be necessary to obtain admittance into said church". The village of Omar has vanished, leaving the 1842 church and cemetery to mark the site of this ghost town. The old meeting house, retaining its original appearance both within and without, is considered one of the finest examples of porticoed Greek Revival architecture, and earned a place on the National Register of Historic Places in 1988. The chapel is still used for Memorial Day services and an occasional funeral, and the cemetery adjoining the chapel is the final resting place of many veterans of early wars, including Aaron Dean, a veteran of the Revolutionary War.

For those preferring not to travel as far as Omar, a short cut is provided on the map. As always, extra caution is advised in those few instances when it is necessary to cross or travel along a state route.

POINTS OF INTEREST:

1. **Monroeville, Ohio**
   The loop begins in the town of Monroeville, where an unusual octagonal house can be seen as you look north from the downtown intersection of Routes 20 & 547. As you travel through town on Monroe, you will pass several interesting structures, including the Zion Episcopal Church at Ridge St. and Monroe St. Built in 1860, it is on the National Register of Historic Places.

2. **St. Peter's Lutheran Church**
   This simple country church dates to 1860, when it was built at a cost of $800.

160

3. St. Sebastian Church

This beautiful country church was erected by Sanguinist Father Kreusch in 1857, replacing a log house that had been previously used. Beneath the new stone-like exterior is the original brick church. Across the street and beside the church stand two other well-preserved houses of the 1850's.

4. Firelands Border

You will be crossing the western border of the Firelands at the jog at the county line. (For more information on the Firelands, see Loop #38.) Use caution on state routes 162 and 4.

5. Omar Chapel & Cemetery

Revolutionary War veteran Aaron Dean is buried near the rear of the cemetery behind the chapel.

6. Military Trail Marker

This historical marker marks the path of a military road opened here during the War of 1812. The trail is now Boughton Road.

7. Havana, Ohio

An abandoned one-room schoolhouse and general store mark the decline of the formerly bustling town of Havana. The only business left in town, besides the elevator, is the Havana Tavern.

8. Peru Township Hall

The entire township of Peru represents one voting precinct, and this simple brick building is the election house and seat of the township government. An early cemetery is located beside the township hall.

9. Grave of Civil War Veteran

Travelers passing this spot before the corn is up in the summer will notice a solitary flag waving in the farm field. It marks the grave of a Civil War veteran, whose gravestone is now gone.

10. Peru, Ohio

This hamlet was a stop on the inland-to-the-lake stagecoach run. The Macksville Tavern, standing alongside the spring, was built in 1836-39, and is now a private residence. It is on the National Register of Historic Places. An early schoolhouse and old brick church can also be seen in Peru, and an early cemetery is located on the north edge of the village.

11. *One-room schoolhouse*

This former one-room schoolhouse has been saved from ruin by its current use as the Monroeville Rod & Gun Club.

12. *Site of Camp Worcester*

In the low-lying fields on the east side of the road was Camp Worcester, where the 3rd Ohio Volunteer Cavalry Regiment camped, drilled, and was mustered into the service of the Union Army in 1861. The regiment went on to see action in such notable battles as Stone River, Chickamauga, and Kenesaw Mountain. A historical plaque can be found on a large boulder along the brick road to the right as you enter Monroeville, and a number of Civil War veterans are buried in the adjoining cemetery.

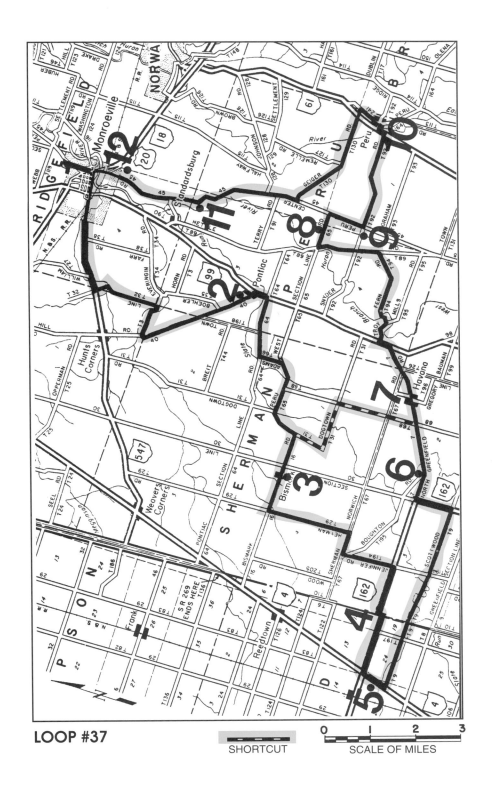

LOOP #37

SHORTCUT

0 1 2 3
SCALE OF MILES

LOOP #38

Length: 50 miles

Terrain: Rolling with a few hills

County: Huron/Ashland/Richland

New Connecticut, Old Order

The backroad explorer in Ohio soon learns that what gives the state its character and fascination is the diversity found within its borders. From the New England style of Ohio's "New Connecticut" to the charm of the horse-drawn wagons of the Amish, this scenic 50 mile tour over the rolling hills of northern Ohio spans two distinct cultures and eras living side-by-side on these buckeye backroads.

The loop begins near the charming town of New London, Ohio, in southeastern Huron county. Known as the "Firelands", this area traces its heritage to the citizens of Connecticut who had been burned out by the British in the Revolutionary War. Colonial Connecticut had claimed all the land lying within her extended borders from "sea to shining sea", and northern Ohio fell within that claim. Over the years, New York and Pennsylvania overlapped this strip, and following the war, Connecticut gave up her claim to most of the rest of the strip that stretched to the western sea. However, she did reserve a portion in northeast Ohio now known as the "Western Reserve", keeping Huron and Erie counties specifically for the fire-sufferers. The money raised by selling the lands of the Reserve was used to seed an educational fund that provides monies for Connecticut schools to this day. In 1800, she finally gave up this little "colony" to Congress, but her imprint remains. The towns in the area bear names such as Greenwich, Plymouth, New Haven, and New London, duplicating the names of the Connecticut homes of many of the early settlers here. The New England influence can still be seen in the architecture of many of the beautiful homes in the countryside and along the streets of the villages.

Leaving the Firelands and heading south, the character of the countryside begins to change, and eventually the smooth road surface gives way to stretches of dirt and gravel. Lines in the dust appear to be tracks left by bicyclists, riding side-by-side, mirroring each other's moves over these quiet backroads of Richland and Ashland counties. But reading between the lines, one sees the tell-tale hoof marks that lead to another era, luring the more adventurous explorer to follow the buggy tracks away from the pace and pavement of the twentieth century. This area is home to the Mennonite and Old Order Amish people, and the traveler will pass by horse-drawn buggies tied to hitching racks at one-room schoolhouses and see draught horses pulling wagon and plow through the fields. You will likely also see horse-drawn vehicles being driven along these roads, so be extra cautious and courteous as you pass through this area.

Following your loop through Amish country, you will back-track over the rolling hills, passing through New London on your way to a swim and picnic at the New London Reservoir.

POINTS OF INTEREST:

1. *New London Reservoir*
   The loop begins here, where parking, swimming, camping, and picnicking are available. Enter from Euclid Road, and begin the loop by heading south from the reservoir. Admission $1.00.

2. *Route Note*
   Use extra caution as you make a left jog across U.S. 224.

3. *Western Reserve Border*
   Your left turn onto C.R. 500 will have you traveling precisely along the southern boundary of the Firelands and old "New Connecticut", known in Ohio as The Western Reserve. If you continued traveling in a straight line eastward to the Atlantic Ocean, you would come to the southern boundary of the present state of Connecticut.

4. *Savannah, Ohio*
   The maroon frame building on the east side of the main street through Savannah is the girls dormitory of the old Savannah Male and Female Academy, dating back to 1865. Tuition for a 40 week term was $10, and residents had to furnish their own bedding and towels. The Academy succumbed to the tax-supported Savannah High School in 1914. On the return leg of the loop, remember to follow Chapel Street out of Savannah.

5. **Amish Schoolhouse**
The lack of electricity leading to this schoolhouse marks it as an Amish schoolhouse, with its outdoor privies and hitching rack.

6. **Fowler Woods State Nature Preserve**
A boardwalk leading back to a buttonbush swamp is but one interesting feature of this preserve. An observation tower is also provided here by the Ohio Department of Natural Resources.

7. **Woodlawn Mennonite Church**
This beautiful brick country church stands out because of its distinctive stone foundation.

8. **Free Road**
As you travel along this gravel road, you will see a large white Mennonite meeting house complete with horse stalls, a Mennonite schoolhouse, and Burkholder's Bulk Food store, open daily except Sunday. Homemade butter is among the goods that can be purchased at this store.

9. **Adario United Methodist Church**

10. **Amish Schoolhouse**

11. **Scenic View**
A spectacular view of farms and towns can be seen as you cross over the hills on this dirt road. Watch out for draught horses crossing the road in this area. For paved, but busy, alternative, proceed east to S.R. 60, then left to Savannah.

12. **New London, Ohio**
Beautiful homes reminiscent of New England line East Main Street as you enter this charming little village. The Connecticut town for which New London is named was burned by Benedict Arnold in the Revolutionary War. Ames Sword Co., the nation's only manufacturer of swords, is located at James and Railroad St. and offers free tours M-F 9-3 (closed first two weeks of July). You may wish to pick up picnic supplies in town before heading for a swim and picnic at the New London Reservoir.

13. **Route Note**
Caution: Steep grade at railroad crossing.

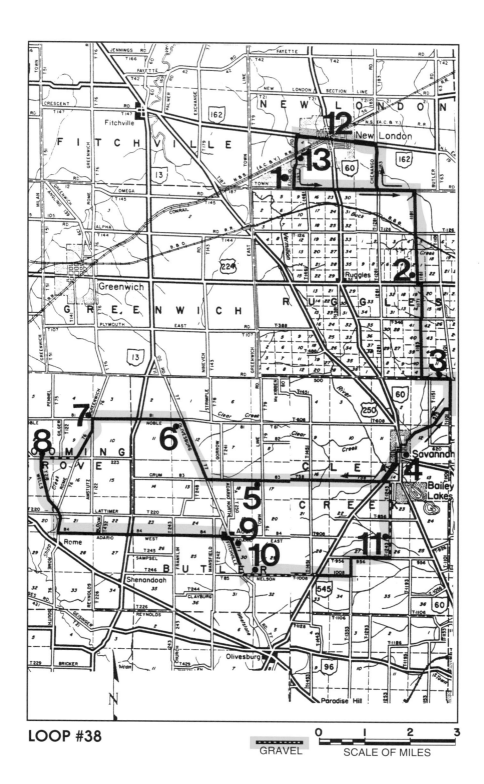

LOOP #38

GRAVEL

0   1   2   3

SCALE OF MILES

LOOP #39

Length: 41 miles

Terrain: Gently rolling to very hilly

County: Ashland/Richland

Malabar Farm

This sojourn from beautiful Mohican State Park passes through broad valleys and over steep hills, offering sweeping views of magnificent countryside. Dairy farms nestling in valleys, iron bridges spanning rushing streams, old stagecoach inns attending winding roads, and country churches hidden in the pines all grace the landscape of this ride through Ashland and Richland Counties. Yet, with all the charming touches that man has added over the years, the landscape itself is the dominant theme. Ralph Waldo Emerson suggested that it was the landscape that was the best part of a farm, and indeed, a case can be made that while the land provides food for the body, the landscape offers food for the soul. The rugged stream-carved valleys of the Mohican River, just beyond the reach of the glacier's softening touch, give way to gentle slopes and contours as we travel through the aptly named Pleasant Valley on our way to Malabar Farm, a farm that is as graceful as the countryside.

Malabar Farm is the storied creation of the late Pulitzer-prize winning novelist, Louis Bromfield. After spending his boyhood on a farm in Ohio, Bromfield went to Europe, and eventually became part of the Paris literary scene. Although likened at one time to such great writers as Hemingway, Bromfield's greatest work was not to be a novel, but would instead be the crafting of a farm in Ohio. After living abroad for many years, he returned home to Pleasant Valley in 1939, and found it to be one of the most beautiful places on earth. He bought four worn-out farms, and, applying principles of farming which he considered in harmony with nature, brought them back to life as Malabar Farm, named for a place in India that he loved. Instituting new methods of agriculture, his farm attracted agricultural experts and "dirt farmers" from all over the world. Among his innovations, he used contour farming, where crops are planted around the hills rather than up and down. Wide green strips of meadow sod catch and hold the rainfall and the topsoil that would otherwise run off into the streams and rivers. His love of the arts is evident at Malabar, for his farming was not concerned with production alone, but also with the beauty of the farmscape.

In Bromfield's book, *Out of the Earth,* he wrote "a lot of things have changed on the farm of today, but the essence of the farm and open countryside remains the same...The farmer may leave his stamp upon the whole of the landscape seen from his window, and it can be as great and beautiful a creation as Michaelangelo's David, for the farmer who takes over a desolate farm, ruined by some ignorant predecessor, and turns it into a paradise of beauty and abundance is one of the greatest of artists." Bromfield sought to share his masterpiece at Malabar with others, and among the thousands who visited during his lifetime were his friends, Humphrey Bogart and Lauren Bacall, who married at the farm in a famous wedding ceremony.

Louis Bromfield wrote five books about his life at Malabar before his death in 1956 at age 59. Today, through the protection and management of the state of Ohio, Malabar Farm lives on as a unique state park. The hills are wrapped with strips of corn and wheat, farm animals roam the pastures, and the "Big House", with the celebrated honeymoon suite, has been preserved as it was in Bromfield's time.

Liberty Hyde Bailey, in *The Holy Earth,* wrote, "To put the best expression of any landscape into the consciousness of one's day...is more to be desired than much riches." From the hills of Mohican to the farm at Malabar, the landscape on this loop paints a picture worth its weight in gold.

POINTS OF INTEREST:

1. *Mohican State Park*
   The loop begins at the picnic facilities at the Class A campground entrance on S.R. 3. (Use caution leaving and returning to the park on S.R. 3.) The park offers a wide range of services, including a variety of campgrounds, cabins, a lodge, and hiking trails. The main park entrance is located on S.R. 97 west of S.R. 3. Reservations for camping are suggested.

2. *Loudonville, Ohio*

The loop makes a left turn in Loudonville at Main St. However, to see the interesting streetscape of downtown Loudonville, make a short side trip to the right at the intersection.

3. *McFall Pioneer Cemetery*

The graves of three veterans of the War of 1812 are found here.

4. *Pleasant Hill Lake*

Restrooms and picnic tables are available at the scenic Pleasant Hill Lake Dam, located almost exactly on the line between glaciated land to the north and west and non-glaciated land to the southeast. Clear Fork Gorge below the dam has been designated a National Natural Landmark, and hiking trails into the gorge are found at the dam. The Morning Glory Spillway is shaped like the flower, hence its name.

5. *Route Note*

Use extra caution on S.R. 95 and 603.

6. *Malabar Inn*

A former stagecoach inn on the run from Cleveland to Marietta, this inn was built in 1820 beside the Niman Spring, which determined the location of the inn. The spring still flows, providing water for ponds and livestock. The restaurant in the Inn has seasonal hours.

7. *Malabar Farm State Park*

Open year-round, the park offers hiking trails, a picnic area, and horsemen's camp, in addition to some farming operations. Stroll around the grounds, pet the animals, or take a wagon tour (offered Wed.-Sun. in summer). Tours of the "Big House" are offered Tues.-Sun., with a charge for the house tour.

8. *Pleasant Valley Lutheran Church*

This quaint brick church was built in 1866.

9. *Newville Baptist Church*

This white frame church, named for the town which disappeared with the construction of the Pleasant Hill Dam, is beautiful in its simplicity.

10. **Butler, Ohio**

The loop makes a "spur" to the little town of Butler, where food and drink are available.

11. **Rummell Mill**

Located by an old metal bridge a short distance from S.R. 95 on a gravel road, this mill was the last in Richland County. It is on the National Register of Historic Places.

12. **Route Note**

A mile and a half stretch of gravel road, passing through a wide scenic valley, lies ahead on Tugend Road (see the dashed line on map). For travelers wishing to avoid this stretch, backtrack to S.R. 95, north to Pleasant Hill, and down McCurdy to pick up the loop at the intersection of Tugend and McCurdy, or follow the busier S.R. 97 east to McCurdy, then right.

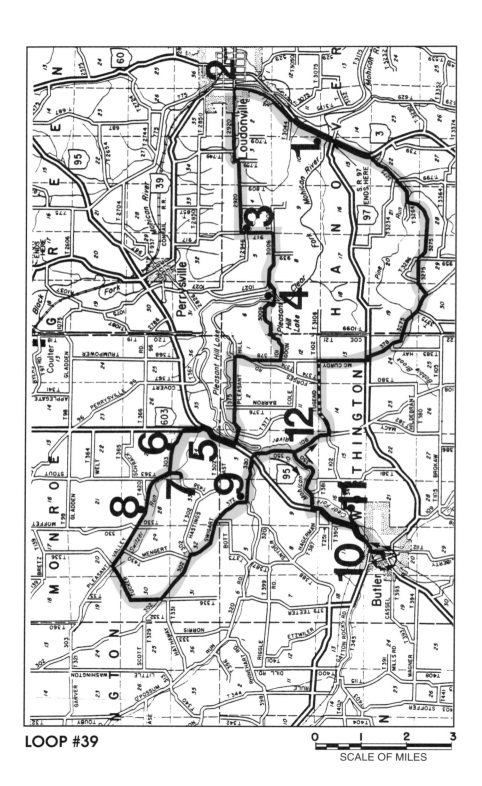

LOOP #39

0   1   2   3

SCALE OF MILES

LOOP #40

Length: 30 miles

Terrain: Gently rolling

County: Medina/Wayne

A Pasture Primer

This outing into the tranquil countryside of northeast Ohio takes the traveler through two small Medina County towns, one reminiscent of a Norman Rockwell painting, the other like a New England village, before heading into the gently rolling dairyland of Wayne County, its green pastures home to herds of black and white dairy cows. Quiet back roads, stately Western Reserve architecture, an occasional horse drawn buggy, and beautiful farms round out this trip through Ohio's foremost dairy region.

When one thinks of a farm, probably the first animal that comes to mind is the cow. We all grew up with them, if only in nursery rhymes, and they are reassuringly familiar to us. From early childhood, we learn that old MacDonald had one on his farm, and that another one jumped over the moon. Often used as a symbol of contentment, there are few creatures that represent peace and tranquility better than a cow, lying in the shade on a hot summer day, absent-mindedly chewing her cud. Often called "Bossy", the term comes not from her temperament, but from the Latin word bos, which means cow. On New Year's Day, 1901, Mr. T. B. Nichols took the podium to address the Ohio Farmers Institute on the practice of raising cows. "There are two distinct breeds of cattle, the dairy and the beef," he said. "The dual purpose cow is a myth. Life is too short to learn everything!"

The most prevalent cow on this loop is the holstein, the black and white cow popular for the large quantity of milk it produces, a milk low in fat. The Holstein originated in Holland, and was imported to the United States by the Dutch in the 1600's. A docile animal, she is the largest of the dairy cows, weighing in at 1,500 pounds. Her black and white color pattern is variable, and the amount of either color can vary widely.

Another popular cow in Ohio, although not as numerous as the Holstein, is the Guernsey, a light tan or even yellowish cow with white patches and a light colored nose. She yields a yellow milk high in fat, known as "Golden Guernsey". The Guernsey is named for an isle in the English Channel, and she came to New England in the early 1800's.

The Jersey cow, cream or light brown with or without white patches, is smaller than the Guernsey, and produces a rich milk that is also good for butter making. Like the Guernsey, she originates on an isle in the English Channel. The Jersey is one of the smaller breeds of dairy cow, and because of her butter and milk production, she makes a good family cow.

Finally, the darkest brown cow is the Brown Swiss, popular for her long productive life. She can also be identified by her black horn tips. She hails originally from Switzerland, and came to this country in the post-Civil War years.

POINTS OF INTEREST:

1. *Hubbard Valley Lake Park*
   The loop begins at this Medina County park, where parking, picnicking, and hiking trails are available. During the summer, boat rentals and refreshments are available from 7 A.M. to dark, Fri.-Sun.

2. *Mound Hill Cemetery*
   The graves of the Kentucky giant, Capt. M.V. Bates, and his wife, Anna Swan Bates, are found in this cemetery. Capt. Bates, an officer in the Confederate Army, was 7'9" tall, and weighed 470 pounds. Still, he had to look up to his wife, who stood 7'11". They were in the P.T. Barnum circus, and afterwards moved to Seville. To visit the monument, enter the east driveway into the cemetery.

3. *Seville, Ohio*
   This friendly small town, once a stagecoach stop on the Cleveland to Cincinnati line, boasts the Seville Inn, an old stagecoach stop that has hosted such notables as President Taft and Archibald Willard, the painter of the famous "Spirit of '76". And, yes, there is a barber of Seville. The tour loops back through town near the end of the ride, so you can choose to explore it now or later. If you happen to be passing through town on the first Sunday of the month between 12:00 and 5:00 (except Dec.-Feb.), you can visit the Seville Historical Society museum. To leave Seville, follow county road 46 at the curve west of the downtown area.

4. Hulburt Homestead

This private residence, now on the National Register of Historic Places, was once the home of Halsey Hulburt. In the election of 1840, Hulbert was one of three anti-slavery electors in Westfield Township, and the home offered refuge to several fugitive slaves.

5. Westfield Center

Formerly known as Le Roy, this button-down village with its town square is much like a proper New England town. The Universalist Church, casting a watchful eye on the square from the north side, is on the National Register of Historic Places. It was erected on this site in 1848. The orderliness of this community can be traced back to the building on the east side of the square, the old offices of the Ohio Farmers Insurance Company, chartered in 1848. It was the first insurance company in the state to insure only farm property, and was headquartered in Le Roy.

6. Western Reserve Border

Where the pavement changes slightly in color on the curve here, one leaves the area formerly known as "New Connecticut" and enters Wayne County, Ohio's leading dairy producer. (For more information about "New Connecticut", see Loop #38.)

7. Canaan, Ohio

Travelers interested in old churches will want to see the U.M. Church here, located on S.R. 604 just east of Canaan Center Road. Several structures of interesting design are located near this crossroads.

8. Hermanville Store

This old store building, with its boom town front, is now a quilt store.

9. Creston Livestock Sales (side trip)

Open only on Mondays, visitors can walk the catwalks above the pens, then watch the auction that begins at 11:30. A snack bar is available.

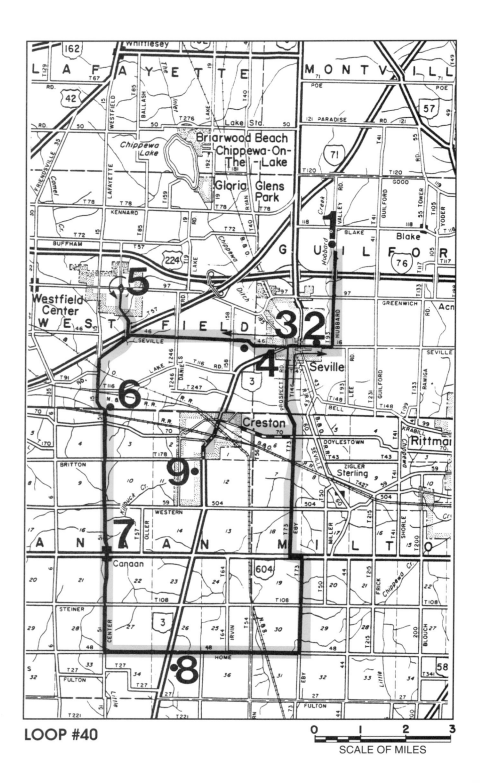

LOOP #40

0   1   2   3
SCALE OF MILES

LOOP #41

Length: 17 miles

Terrain: Gently rolling with one steep hill

County: Summit

The Ohio & Erie Canal

"To the Ohio Canal, serpentine in its course, embracing within its coils the most productive regions of Hog and Hominy." So rang out the farmers' toast on July 4, 1827 to the dawn of a new era in Ohio, for the first leg of the Ohio & Erie Canal, stretching from Akron to Cleveland, was complete. The markets of New York and beyond were now open to the pork and grain of the Ohio farmers, and instead of a festering backwater hidden from the world, Ohio made a giant leap toward growth and commerce. This loop through the valley of the Cuyahoga River in Summit County takes us back to those days of the old canal, where we can walk the towpaths and marvel at the massive stone locks and aqueduct abutments, old stone quarries and scattered millstones that draw us into an era of achievement and celebration a century and a half ago. A charming canal era town, a restored pioneer village and a beautiful covered bridge round out this journey through the southern end of the Cuyahoga Valley National Recreation Area, Ohio's only national park.

Independence Day was the customary date for celebrations and great events in those early days of the republic, and it was on Independence Day in 1825 that ground was broken for the Ohio & Erie Canal, a forty foot wide ditch that was to eventually carry a ribbon of water 308 miles long from the Ohio River at Portsmouth to Lake Erie at Cleveland. The canal from Cleveland to Akron (which means "high place") had to ascend 395 feet to its summit, so a staircase of water had to be constructed. The steps in this staircase were the locks, and 44 locks were needed in this stairway to Akron. Each lock was a stone chamber 90 feet long and 15 feet wide, with wooden gates at either end that would open and close, allowing the lock to fill with water, lifting the southbound boats, and empty, lowering the northbound boats. Water at slow times was directed around the lock in a race, and often mills sprang up at these sites to take advantage of this water power.

The locks were not the only engineering feat that had to be accomplished along the canal's course. Just as it is necessary for highway bridges to carry modern roads over rivers and streams, it was necessary in places for aqueducts to carry the canal. Instead of pavement, though, this roadway of water was carried over river and stream in a trough, or flume. Perpetually leaking, they were the source of much lost water in the summer, and much icicle beauty in the winter.

More than 150 years has gone by since the first canal boat, *The State of Ohio,* passed through here, touching off massive celebrations. As we emerge from the towpath trail in the shadow of a stately railroad bridge and begin our journey along these backroads, we are in a very real sense fulfilling the dreams of those celebrating men who raised their glasses in a series of toasts on that July 4, 1827. "To the President of the United States," they drank, then "to General George Washington", "to domestic manufacture", "to Bunker Hill", "to the arrival of the first boat on the Ohio Canal", and prophetically, "to canals and roads—may their construction progress until boats may glide and wheels roll unobstructed to every part of the American Continent". And may we add today, "to the Canal Builders of Ohio!".

POINTS OF INTEREST:

1. *Deep Lock Quarry Park*
   The loop begins at this Akron Metropolitan park, where parking and picnic tables are provided. Four generations of transportation huddle in this valley: the river, the canal, the railroad, and today's roadway. Follow the towpath foot trail to magnificent Deep Lock, the deepest lock on the entire canal. Its lift of 17 feet doubled the average lock's lift of 8-10 feet. As you hike the 1.2 mile trail that runs between the old canal channel and the Cuyahoga River, you will pass huge millstones scattered along the way. The same trail leads to the abandoned Deep Lock Quarry where the millstones and the stones for the locks were quarried.

2. *Johnny Cake Lock*
   This lock derives its name from the fried cornbread fed to passengers stranded here when their boat ran aground in the mud. The house standing beside the lock was an inn and possibly served as a lockmaster's house. The brush-choked lock is located behind and just north of the ranger's headquarters at Everett Road and Riverview Road.

3. Everett Covered Bridge

The last remaining covered bridge in the Cuyahoga Valley, this bridge was restored in 1986 by the National Park Service after its near destruction in a flood on May 21, 1975. Its date of first construction is less precise. According to the Park Service, the bridge was born of tragedy when, on February 1, 1877, John Gillson perished in the swirling icy waters trying to rescue his wife, who was saved by local residents. The death of Mr. Gillson led to the construction of the bridge, eliminating the necessity and danger of fording the stream. Other sources indicate the bridge was built as early as 1856. The bridge is open to non-vehicular traffic, and bicyclists wishing to avoid a steep climb and descent can take a short-cut here to Hale Farm.

4. Hale Farm and Village

Located on the homestead of Jonathon Hale, one of the valley's earliest settlers, this living history museum is open June through October, Wed.-Sat. 10-5, Sun. 12-5. Closed first two weeks of September. Admission charge.

5. Ira Cemetery

The grave markers of Jonathon Hale and John Gillson can be found in this small pioneer cemetery.

6. Peninsula, Ohio

So named because of the bend in the river, this charming canal-era town is home to beautiful old churches, schools, and homes. By walking north along the railroad tracks past the old depot to the bend in the river, you can see the stone abutments of the old Peninsula Aqueduct that carried the canal across the river. The Moody and Thomas Mill stood at the south end of the aqueduct on the inside of the bend. Food and drink are available in Peninsula, and Fisher's Cafe has a large number of interesting canal-era photographs displayed on the walls.

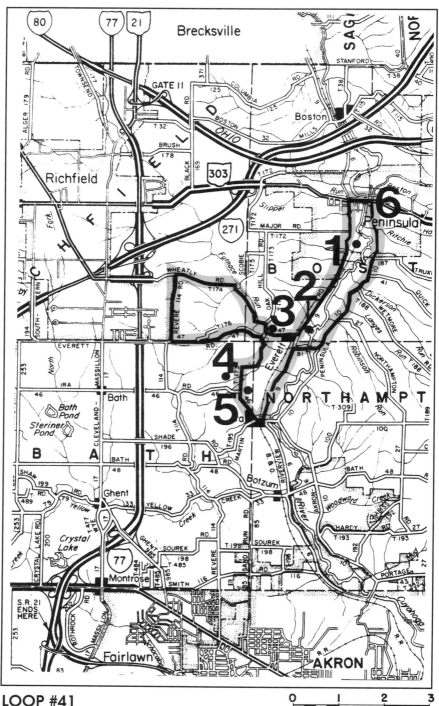

LOOP #41

0   1   2   3

SCALE OF MILES

LOOP #42

Length: 48 miles

Terrain: Gently rolling

County: Ashtabula

Covered Bridge Country

This tour over the rolling terrain of Ashtabula County takes the traveler into the heart of Ohio's covered bridge country. Located in Ohio's most northeasterly county, this loop features eight of the county's fourteen covered bridges, and includes the newest covered bridge in the state. While time is sweeping many of Ohio's covered bridges into the past, Ashtabula County has actually seen an increase in the number of her covered bridges over the past few years.

As the twentieth century dawned, the old timber spans were giving way to iron and steel construction, then later to pre-stressed concrete decks and guardrails. Since around 1920, there had not been a single authentic covered bridge built in Ohio, and the skills of the great bridge builders of the 1800's were slipping away with their bridges. Men like Reuben Partridge of Union County, who built more than 200 bridges in Ohio in the nineteenth century before falling from a bridge to his death at age 77, and Everett Sherman of Preble County, seemed to have taken their skills and knowledge with them. But tucked away in the corner of the state in Ashtabula County is a man who is following in the footsteps of the early builders of Ohio. County Engineer John Smolen has not only restored and strengthened many of the county's century-old covered bridges, he actually built two new covered bridges in the 1980's. His magnificent State Road Covered Bridge, built in 1983, was the first certified authentic covered bridge built in Ohio in 63 years. He followed this with the Caine Road Covered Bridge in 1986, making that span the newest covered bridge in Ohio today.

Being the first covered bridge built in Ohio in more than half a century, the construction of the State Road Covered Bridge naturally drew the interest of hundreds, then thousands, of people. The huge bridge was built on the roadway, then slowly moved into position over the creek. Pulling with a winch and

pushing with a bulldozer, the move took three weeks to complete, and with the bridge finally in place, Ohio had once again
entered the covered bridge era. One can't help but think that
somewhere in the crowd that summer day at Conneaut Creek
were two old bridge builders, watching with twinkling eyes, and
maybe even helping, the State Road Covered Bridge slide into
its place over the creek and into history.

POINTS OF INTEREST:

1. *Jefferson, Ohio*
   The loop begins in Jefferson, the county seat of Ashtabula
   County. As part of "New Connecticut", the town boasts a number of beautiful early churches and New England style homes
   along Jefferson St. Turn right at Poplar St. from W. Jefferson St. to
   follow the loop.

2. *Doyle Road Covered Bridge*
   This beautiful bridge was built in 1868, and restored in 1988. It has
   several features that you will find in some of the other bridges on
   this loop. The massive arches in the bridge, called Burr arches,
   serve to increase the load capacity of the span. Patented in
   1804 by Theodore Burr, they were sometimes built into a bridge's
   original construction, and sometimes added later. The design of
   the bridge is called the Town Lattice, named for Ithiel Town, who
   patented the design. It was first used around 1820, and was a
   cost effective yet strong design for bridges of this length.

3. *Olin Covered Bridge*
   Located on Dewey Road, this Town Lattice bridge was built in
   1873 by a Mr. Potter over the Ashtabula River.

4. *Benetka Road Covered Bridge*
   This Town Lattice bridge was probably built in the 1890's. The Burr
   arches, consisting of 37 boards glued and nailed together, were
   added in 1985, and served to quadruple the bridge's load
   capacity.

5. *Gageville Country Store*
   This country store is housed in the old Gageville Methodist
   Church, built in 1844. Open seven days a week, you may wish to
   stop here for refreshments. Use extra caution as you travel north
   along S.R. 193 for about a mile.

6. State Road Covered Bridge

Located in a beautiful setting over Conneaut Creek, this magnificent covered bridge was built in 1983 by John Smolen. The slight "camel back" of the bridge is to facilitate draining. After visiting the bridge, turn around and backtrack southward to continue the loop.

7. Kelloggsville Stagecoach Inn

Built in 1824 by Caleb Blodgett, the Kelloggsville Stagecoach Inn served the coach traffic along the Stanhope-Kelloggsville Road, a road that Blodgett also built. Called the town's "leading business spirit", he came here from Vermont in 1810 and established several distilleries and mills. The old brick inn is now a private residence.

8. Root Road Covered Bridge

This bridge was built in 1868, and the wooden "girders" along the sides inside the bridge were added recently to strengthen the span.

9. Graham Road Covered Bridge

This well-traveled covered bridge was built on Graham Road from the remains of a bridge washed downstream from Pierpont in the flood of 1913. By-passed in 1971, the bridge is now the centerpiece of a small park located by a riffling stream, and a picnic table can be found in the cool shade within the bridge. It is another Town Lattice bridge.

10. Caine Road Covered Bridge

Built in 1986 by John Smolen, this is the newest covered bridge in Ohio.

11. South Denmark Covered Bridge

Although this bridge was by-passed in 1975, automobiles may still drive through it by following the gravel drive that leads to the bridge. Built in 1895, it is yet another Town Lattice bridge.

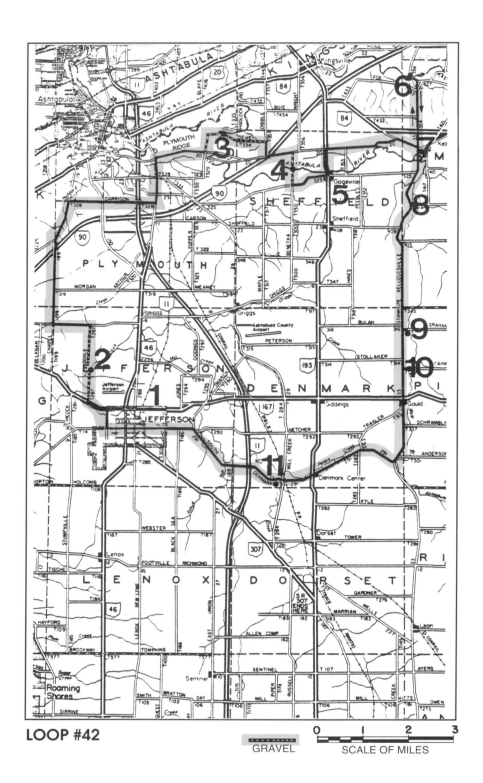

LOOP #42

GRAVEL

SCALE OF MILES

0   1   2   3

SECTION V. *Ohio Hill Country*

McCoppin's Mill. Loop #45

Trip Planning Guide
Ohio Hills

# Name	Length (miles)	Historical site	Nature preserve	Museum	Covered bridge(s)	Pioneer cemetery	Picnic area	Camping (state/county park)	Swimming	Walking trails
43. Plymouth Street, 1837	32	X			X	X	X	X	X	
44. The Sandy and Beaver Canal	36	X		X	X		X	X	X	X
45. Mounds of Mystery	49	X	X	X			X	X	X	X
46. Appalachian Way	49	X	X	X	X	X	X	X	X	X
47. Hocking Hills	51		X				X	X	X	X
48. Paint Valley Pilgrimage	52	X		X	X	X	X	X	X	X
49. Perry Pride	40	X					X	X		
50. One for the Road	56	X		X	X		X	X	X	X

A Note to Bicyclists: Because of the rugged terrain in the Ohio Hills, the occasional gravel road is unavoidable. Road and traffic conditions vary greatly, and busier state routes are sometimes the only reasonable option. Shorter sight lines and steep grades are other hazards for the cyclist. Because of these conditions, we advise cyclists to undertake these tours only at their own risk, and to enjoy them by car before deciding to cycle.

Tour Loop Locations
Ohio Hills

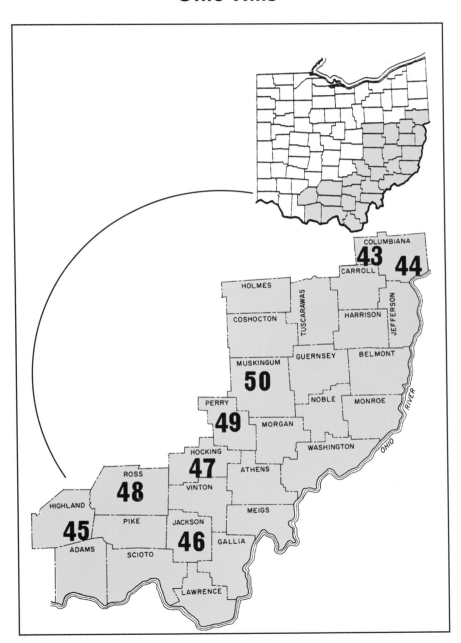

LOOP #43

Length: 32 miles

Terrain: Rolling to hilly

County: Columbiana

Plymouth Street, 1837

As the crow flies, the trip from Guilford Lake State Park to Hanoverton is about three miles and takes about ten minutes. In keeping with our slow lane tradition, we make this short trip into a trek of about 32 miles and go back in time more than 150 years. On the way to Hanoverton we will pass through covered bridges, ride along scenic ridges, visit a log cabin shrine, see beautiful old churches, and stop at a historic cemetery. For travelers who work up an appetite or thirst along the way, food and drink are available at a canal era tavern in Hanoverton.

This rolling area of Columbiana County hearkens back to the days of the Sandy & Beaver Canal, and one of those bustling towns that welcomed canal travelers in the 1830's quietly welcomes travelers today along the canal's abandoned course. Located at the west end of the now collapsed Big Tunnel, an enormous canal project that bored through Tunnel Hill between Dungannon and Hanoverton, Hanoverton's Plymouth Street looks much the same as it did 150 years ago. The brick buildings and homes along the narrow shady street date back to the early 1800's, and nearly two dozen of them bear plaques indicating that they are on the National Register of Historic Places.

Hanoverton was founded as Hanover in 1813 by Quaker James Craig about a decade before Ohio's canal era began. It served as a stop on the underground railroad, and its population burgeoned to 2,000 in the 1830's. Financial disaster struck the nation in 1837, and the Panic of 1837 spelled delay for the canal and unemployment for the canal builders. Fortunately for many of the workers, Will Rhodes needed help in building a tavern and inn that year on Plymouth Street. The Spread Eagle Tavern, a splendid example of Federal architecture with eleven rooms and a dozen fireplaces, was inspired by the work of the gifted eighteenth century architect Asher Benjamin. The tavern was visited by several notables, chief among them Abraham Lincoln. The grand life of Hanover was short, though, and when the railroads supplanted the canal, the town languished.

Today, the town is called Hanoverton, the canal is gone, but the rebuilt and restored Spread Eagle Tavern is open for business, offering food and lodging to travelers along historic Plymouth Street.

To visit more features of the canal in this area, please see "The Sandy & Beaver Canal" tour.

POINTS OF INTEREST:

1. *Guilford Lake State Park*
   The centerpiece of this state park is Guilford Lake, built around 1835 to supply water to the ill-fated Sandy & Beaver Canal. When the canal was abandoned in 1852, the reservoir dried up. Seventy-five years later the state acquired the property and restored the lake by impounding the waters of the West Fork of Little Beaver Creek . Today, camping, fishing, swimming and picnicking are popular activities at Guilford Lake. The loop begins at the picnic area on the east side of the reservoir.

2. *Teegarden Covered Bridge*
   This multiple kingpost covered bridge was built in 1876, and carries travelers across the Middle Fork of Little Beaver Creek.

3. *Miller Covered Bridge*
   Another multiple kingpost covered bridge, this span across Mill Site Creek is only 37 feet long. It dates back to 1860.

4. *Route Note*
   S.R. 164 in and out of Lisbon is a state-designated scenic route. It carries fast-moving traffic, and is selected because there are no reasonable paved alternatives. Use extra caution.

5. *Lisbon, Ohio*
   This charming town has retained many of its early brick buildings. As you pass through on S.R. 164, you will see on the northeast corner of Market and Park Sts. the Sandy and Beaver Insurance Company. That brick building was the birthplace of Marcus Hanna, William McKinley's manager and "the closest thing this country ever had to a political boss." Turn right on W. Lincoln Way, then left at the light onto S. Lincoln to follow the route. Just a few houses beyond the turn on W. Lincoln is the birthplace of Clement Vallandigham. Vallandigham, a fiery Ohio politician and leader of the Copperheads, was banished to the Confederacy

by Lincoln for speeches sympathetic to the South. His birthplace is at 431 W. Lincoln Way, a highway named for his old nemesis.

6. New Lebanon U.P. Church

Located in a peaceful scenic valley, the architecture of this simple church reflects the New England design common to many area churches.

7. St. Paul's Cemetery

Visitors to the cemetery will notice a square free of gravestones where the first Catholic parish in northern Ohio was situated. Also of interest is the large marker of Rev. Lindesmith, former Army Chaplain and veteran of the Indian Wars in the Rockies in the 1880's. On the back of the monument is a listing of dozens of relatives, probably the most extensive listing of relatives on a marker in Ohio.

8. Log Cabin Shrine of Dungannon

Moved to Dungannon from its original site in St. Paul's Cemetery, this log cabin was the birthplace of Catholicism in northern Ohio. The steeple looming large behind the cabin reflects the growth of the church in the ensuing century and a half.

9. Canal Tunnel Hill

Although our route over the hill between Dungannon and Hanoverton is quiet today, travelers on January 7, 1848 were accompanied by a brass band celebrating the opening of the canal tunnel that ran through the hill. In fact, the music was so loud that it nearly deafened the passengers, and caused a rock to crash into their path in the channel. It was the only concert ever offered in tunnel hill!

10. Canal Tunnel Historical Marker

A short distance to the right on Route 30 is a historical marker describing Big and Little Tunnels, the only canal tunnels in Ohio. The tunnels are a monument to the labor of the Irish who used hand drills and blasting powder to bore more than 1,000 yards through the hill. A gravel pulloff is found just short of the marker. Use caution.

11. Hanoverton, Ohio

Turn right onto Plymouth St. to pass through this charming old canal town. Turn right on Clinton St. to leave town. Please see the narrative for information.

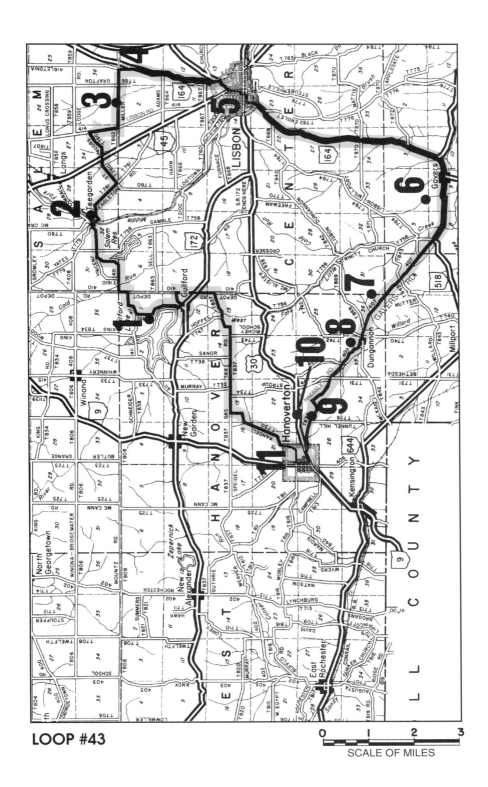

LOOP #43

0   1   2   3

SCALE OF MILES

LOOP #44

Length: 36 miles

Terrain: Very hilly!

County: Columbiana

The Sandy and Beaver Canal

Works of both man and nature grace this spectacular sojourn through the valley of Little Beaver Creek in Columbiana County. Travelers unfamiliar with the wild and rugged terrain of Ohio's hill country will imagine themselves in another region as they gaze down from scenic overlooks upon deep cut valleys and meandering streams, railroad trestles and roads appearing in miniature far below. The untamed terrain shows no evidence of the glaciers that smoothed and filled much of the rest of Ohio, for it was here that the powerful ice sheet stalled, unable to further its advance across the state. The misty valley of Little Beaver Creek is where the line was drawn, and is the setting of this 36 mile loop from Little Beaver State Park. Nestled in the valley are old mills, metal bridges, historic towns, and remnants of a grand but ill-fated undertaking—the Sandy & Beaver Canal.

Canal fever hit the state with the passage of the Canal Act of 1825, and rays of hope found their way into the back country where Ohio farmers and artisans were in need of markets for their wares. In east-central Ohio, the Sandy & Beaver Canal was proposed as a feeder canal to tie into the Ohio & Erie Canal and into the Pennsylvania market via the Ohio River, passing through relatively unsettled land. Construction commenced in 1834 under the supervision of Edward Gill, a consummate craftsman himself.

Under Gill's guidance, superb workmanship was the watchword. Unfortunately, financial trouble hit the country in 1837, and Gill, rather than suffer "cheap" engineering, left for other endeavors. The canal eventually was completed after a seven year hiatus, with the eastern division, through which our tour passes, comprising 27 miles with 57 locks, among them Gill's magnificent works. The summit level just to the west required two tunnels to be constructed through hills, a daunting challenge that was to prove extremely time consuming. By the time the canal was completed, the railroad was bearing down on the project. After only two years of operation, a reservoir breach and the steel rails spelled the end of the Sandy & Beaver.

The canal in this area tied together the towns of Sprucevale, Williamsport, Elkton and others, some of which are now just ghost towns. And in a similar vein, tales have sprung up along the old canal of haunted mills and locks. Is the mist in the valley simply playing tricks—or could the old canal be haunted? We will let the traveler decide!

For those wishing to explore a nearby canal era town on the old summit level, please see the "Plymouth Street, 1837" loop.

POINTS OF INTEREST:

1. *Sprucevale*
   Once a town along the canal, this ghost town is located at the group camp and picnic area of Beaver Creek State Park. A magnificent stone mill, built in 1813 by James Hambleton, stands across the road from the Hambleton Lock. Gretchen's Lock is found 1/2 mile down the trail from the end of the parking lot. Legend has it that it served as a temporary tomb for Gretchen, Edward Gill's daughter, and those who maintain the trail insist that it is haunted. Hard-bitten realists insist that Gill had no children. (Family camping is available elsewhere in the park.)

2. *Pretty Boy Floyd*
   Pretty Boy Floyd met his match at the hands of lawmen here on October 22, 1934. Newspapers reported that "he lived like he died, with the echo of gunfire reverberating in his ears." To stand on the spot, turn left on a grassy drive in a field about 100 feet before reaching the horsemen's camp. About midway along this U shaped drive is an apple tree, and about 15 feet to the left of the tree is a flat unmarked stone marking the spot where Charles "Pretty Boy" Floyd died.

3. *Clarkson Presbyterian Church*
   This white frame church, established in 1839, is in the New England style of architecture. Turn left at the church.

4. *Beaver Creek State Park's Pioneer Village*
   Cross the beautiful metal truss bridge to visit Pioneer Village. The highlights of the village are the restored Lock 36, complete with wooden gates and sweeps, and Gaston's Mill, built in 1830. The

Thomas J. Malone Covered Bridge, built in 1870, has been moved to this site, and other early log buildings house a blacksmith shop and chapel. The buildings are open weekend afternoons in the summer. A hiking trail that passes more locks can be reached at the end of the metal bridge across the creek from the village. Maps are available at the ranger's office above the village.

5. **Williamsport Chapel**
   This church is another of the white frame churches reminiscent of New England that are common to the area.

6. **Lusk's Lock**
   Technically Lock 27 on the Eastern Division of the canal, this beautifully crafted structure is called Lusk's Lock in honor of one of the contractors. Gill's perfectionism shines through with the stairways that spiral up the lock on the far end. The stairs were to assist the boatmen in reaching the sweeps as they negotiated the lock. The lock is located a couple hundred yards down the creekside trail that leads from the parking lot.

7. **Elkton, Ohio**
   This former canal town is home to Lock 24, the ruins of which can be seen behind the Lock 24 Restaurant. Also relocated here is the 1870 Church Hill Road Covered Bridge, one of the shortest covered bridges in the country. A beautiful herb garden grows behind the restaurant.

8. **Fredericktown**
   This tiny town is a step back in time. Turn left off S.R. 170 just past the one-room schoolhouse to see the octagonal building that originally served as a school in 1861, then later as a post office and general store. An 1893 metal bridge crosses the creek beside the foundation of an old mill. Up the hill beyond the bridge is a scenic overlook, marked by a roadside bench. This is a favorite spot for photographers.

9. **Scenic Overlook**

10. **Route Note**
    Turn right on County Rd. 430, then right on 428.

11. **Scenic Overlook**

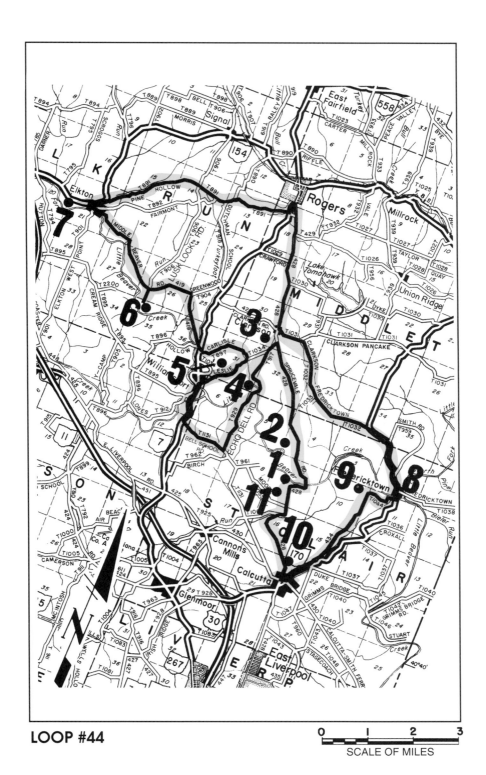

LOOP #44

0   1   2   3
SCALE OF MILES

LOOP #45

Length: 49 miles

Terrain: Rolling to hilly

County: Highland/Adams

Mounds of Mystery

There are few areas as steeped in mystery as the area through which you will be traveling on this loop through Ohio's bluegrass country, a small area of flat-topped hills that is an extension of the Kentucky terrain to the south. Mounds made by both man and meteor are the highlights of this scenic tour from Rocky Fork Lake through Highland and Adams counties, a region unsurpassed in the beauty of its landscape or the depth of its secrets.

Like the proverbial flea on the elephant, it is difficult for us to envision the topography of the land that we are traversing. To most of us, we are simply going up one hill or down another, and the horizon just looks like so many knobs, with neither pattern nor reason. But to some of the people living here, both now and perhaps millennia ago, the area is "different." As one man commented, "things just ain't right around here." Rocks are found out of place, some layers completely upside down and 1,000 feet higher than they should be. Other rocks are 400 feet lower than their nearby counterparts.

By taking a large overview of the area near the Adams and Highland county boundary, it has been learned that a five mile wide circular area, termed a "cryptoexplosion," exists here, an area much like an impression caused by a giant doughnut. There is an outer depressed ring, then another ring that is elevated. The center or hole of the doughnut is even more elevated, rising 950 feet above the normal level.

What caused this massive upheaval? Earlier theories that the sudden release of pent up volcanic gases created the massive structure have given way to the current idea that the area is an "astrobleme," or star wound, caused by a meteor smashing into the earth with massive force more than 325 million years ago. The impact was so devastating that the center actually rebounded 1,000 feet above its original level, while the outer ring remained depressed by the collision.

196

Although the size of this meteor mound makes it difficult for us to grasp, a smaller yet just as perplexing puzzle is found on the southwest side of the cryptoexplosion. Serpent Mound, a mysterious effigy tattooing this star-struck area, lies coiled above Ohio Brush Creek. The snake's quarter mile length is contained in seven deep coils, and its open mouth appears to be swallowing an egg. There is some indication that the snake's alignment relates to astronomical observations, but little is known for certain about the mound or its builders.

Probably built between 1000 B.C. and 700 A.D., the snake likely represented a deep religious or mystical principle for its builders. Was it an evil force or a benevolent deity? Did it represent the renewal of life, as a snake sheds its skin, or, as one early Adams county preacher maintained, does Serpent Mound mark the spot of the Garden of Eden and the fall of man? Others ask if it is a serpent at all, speculating that it is a stylized comet with tail, telling us the story of the star that fell from the sky. Is it possible that the prehistoric mound builders knew something that we do not—and if so, how did they know? Perhaps after your visit to the area, you will have a theory of your own!

POINTS OF INTEREST:

1. **Rocky Fork State Park**
   The tour begins at the picnic area on the east side of the lake. Enjoy the success of the bluebird project here! Tent and RV camping, swimming, and hiking are some of the activities available at the park.

2. **Fort Hill**
   Found atop the steep slopes of this hill is an enclosure of stone and earth built by prehistoric people, probably the Hopewells, that has stood for perhaps 2,000 years. The wall, a little more than a mile and a half in length, encloses 40 hill top acres that may have served as a special area for clan and tribal rituals. Ten miles of hiking trails lead to some of Ohio's most unusual flora, including the elusive Canby's mountain lover and Canadian yew. The area is open year-round during daylight hours, no charge. It is maintained by the Ohio Historical Society.

3. **Edge of Cryptoexplosion**
   The hill south of Sinking Spring marks your entry into the Serpent Mound Cryptoexplosion (see narrative).

4. *Serpent Mound State Memorial*

This Ohio Historical Society site is open daily in the summer, and on weekends in the spring and fall. Admission charge.

(For those wishing to challenge their observational skills, the profile of the cryptoexplosion "doughnut" (see narrative for description) may be discerned on the horizon to the northeast from the Tranquility Wildlife area, which is located just beyond the border of our map. To reach the area, turn left from S.R. 73 onto S.R. 770 about three miles east from Serpent Mound, then south about two miles.)

5. *1893 Metal Bridge*

6. *McCoppin's Mill*

This is the last survivor of a half dozen mills built on Rocky Fork Creek in the 1800's. McCoppin's Mill was built in 1829 and operated until the 1970's. Its scenic location by a beautiful cut-stone dam makes it popular with photographers.

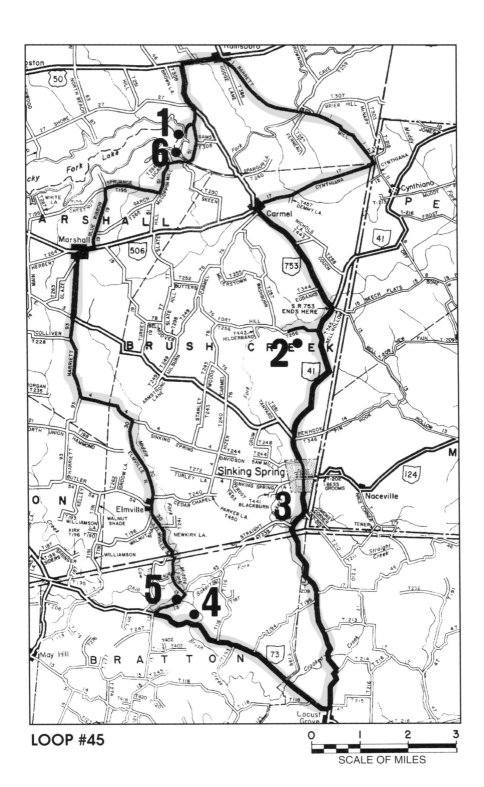

LOOP #45

SCALE OF MILES

0   1   2   3

LOOP #46

Length: 49 miles

Terrain: Mostly valley or ridge roads, some steep hills

County: Jackson

Appalachian Way

The ruggedly beautiful hills of the Allegheny Plateau in southern Ohio is the setting of this trek back in time. Hills and hollows, a restored charcoal iron furnace, prehistoric rock carvings, covered bridges, scenic trails and a hill top cemetery are all part of this trip through Jackson County in Ohio's Appalachia.

Jackson County, situated in an area untouched by the glaciers, represents part of Ohio's oldest landscape. These tree covered hills drew some of Ohio's earliest pioneers, and the original forest, spared by the ice, fell to the advance of man. Smoke hung in the air from the burning piles of logs as farms replaced forest, but the farmers of pioneer days soon learned that the soil was shallow, and as it eroded away, so did their hopes.

Another industry took root here in the mid-1800's, an industry with an insatiable appetite for fuel. Again smoke hung in the valleys, this time from the massive stone furnaces that daily converted an acre of forest into charcoal to make the iron that supplied a growing nation. Hanging Rock, as this region became known, was noted for producing the finest quality iron in the country. Hanging Rock iron went into the rails that were stretching across the land, and into the munitions that saved the Union. Iron for the ironclad *Monitor* came from Jackson County. The town of Wellston was laid out in the heart of the iron region in 1873, and in only a decade grew from a farm to a town of 5,000.

While the charcoal iron industry boomed, life on the "furnace estates" was anything but easy. Centered around the massive stone furnace, life revolved around feeding the furnace and drawing out the molten iron. The molten iron would flow out of the furnace onto the floor of the casting room, where it was channeled into separate "troughs" to harden. Because it resembled a sow with piglets on the casting room floor, the iron was known as pig iron. The workers were poorly paid, and in hard economic times would work just for housing for their families. The company store also held the laborers fast to the furnace, adding further discouragement to an already hard life.

By the 1880's, coke furnaces were replacing the charcoal furnaces, and soon the industry here was dead. The abandoned furnaces decayed, and communities vanished. Today, Buckeye Furnace, built nearly a century and a half ago, has been restored by the Ohio Historical Society, and offers a fascinating look back to those days when Ohio was emerging from its pioneer era into the first days of her industrial age.

Following your visit to Buckeye Furnace, loop back through Wellston for a scenic journey to Leo Petroglyph, prehistoric rock etchings left by Ohio's earliest peoples. Enjoy a spectacular view from a hill top cemetery and a trip through a covered bridge before returning to a picnic and swim at Lake Alma.

POINTS OF INTEREST:

1. **Lake Alma State Park**
   Camping, swimming, hiking and picnicking are offered at this state park.

2. **Route Note**
   To by-pass Wellston's busy downtown area, turn left from S.R. 93 onto E Street, then right on New York to Tenth St., then left out of town.

3. **Buckeye Furnace and Covered Bridge**
   Operated by the Ohio Historical Society, the park is open daily April to October, and the exhibits and store are open Weds.-Sun. Admission charge. (Rough road.)

   Located just beyond the furnace is the Buckeye Furnace Covered Bridge, built in 1872 and still in service over Little Raccoon Creek.

4. **Route Note**
   To follow the scenic tour to Leo Petroglyph, retrace your route through Wellston to Broadway St., turn left and follow Broadway (S.R. 327) through town to #8 Pike, then turn right.

5. *Leo Petroglyph*

Considered some of the finest petroglyphs, or carved writings, in Ohio, these figures of a bird, a fish, an unidentified animal, and three human feet still mystify visitors. The most striking figure is that of a human head or face wearing what appears to be a headdress—or is it antlers? The figures are believed to have been carved by the late Fort Ancient Indians 700 years ago. Other carvings, such as Bob loves Heather, appear to be of more recent vintage. A historical marker is located west of the shelter.

A nature trail loops away from the petroglyph shelter and leads into a deep gorge past several interesting rock formations. Signs along the trail explain many of these features. Open year-round, no charge.

6. *Byer Cemetery and Scenic Overlook*

Turn left from S.R. 327 at the Richland Furnace Forest sign (County Rd. 31) to reach the hill top cemetery and a spectacular view of the valley. Veterans of the Civil War from Ohio and West Virginia companies are among those buried here, and a marker with an anvil on top undoubtedly marks the grave of a blacksmith. Follow the drive down the hill and turn left to continue the loop.

7. *Byer Covered Bridge*

Still carrying traffic over Pigeon Creek, this Smith truss covered bridge was built in 1872.

8. *Route Note*

To return to Lake Alma, retrace the route back to Wellston, then north to the park.

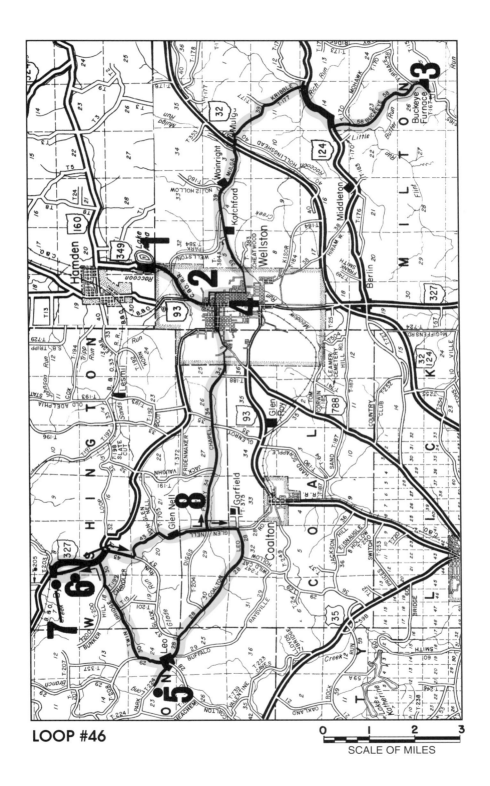

LOOP #46

SCALE OF MILES

0 1 2 3

LOOP # 47

Length: 51 miles

Terrain: Gently rolling to hilly

County: Hocking

The Hocking Hills

Considered one of Ohio's most beautiful regions, the Hocking Hills area represents some of nature's most magnificent and unusual handiwork. Spectacular gorges, wondrous rock bridges, enchanting caves, cliffs and waterfalls grace the route on this scenic tour of the hills of southeast Ohio. The accessibility of most of these points of interest is fairly easy, but for those wishing to hike, be sure to bring your hiking shoes for some of Ohio's best hiking.

Hocking County takes its name from the Indian word Hockhocking, which means bottleneck. According to John White in the *American Pioneer*, "About six or seven miles northwest of Lancaster there is a fall in the Hockhocking River, of about twenty feet: above the fall for a short distance the creek is very narrow and straight, forming a neck, while at the falls it suddenly widens on each side and swells into the appearance of the body of a bottle. The whole, when seen from above, appears exactly in the shape of a bottle, and from this fact the Indians called the creek Hockhocking." The name was shortened later by the settlers to Hocking, as it is known today.

Although the Hocking Hills now attract thousands of people seeking nature's beauty and peace, this area served as a haven for outlaws before the coming of the Hocking Canal and the tourists that came aboard the canal boats. Horse thieves would hide stolen horses in the many caves in the area, and bandits would lay in wait for unsuspecting victims along the trails. Hermits seeking refuge from civilization took up residence in the hollows and caves, and one elderly hermit, Richard Rowe, eventually caused his cave to become known as "Old Man's Cave." Indians held council fires in the recesses, while all the while nature continued her artistry through the forces of water and wind, creating natural wonders unrivaled in Ohio.

The journey through the Hocking Hills is a delight in any season, but the fall colors make it an especially appealing trip in the autumn.

POINTS OF INTEREST:

1. *Lake Logan State Park*
   The tour begins at Lake Logan State Park, named for the Mingo Indian leader Johnny Logan. The park offers parking lots, picnicking, swimming, and restrooms. (For those wishing to camp, campgrounds are available at Old Man's Cave, which is found on this loop.)

2. *Route Note:*
   Use caution on this short stretch of Route 33. It is a divided highway with wide berms.

3. *Rockbridge*
   Turn right on T.R. 124 from Route 33 and follow the signs to Rockbridge State Nature Preserve. The centerpiece of the preserve is the rock bridge, one of only about a dozen such geological features in all of Ohio. This natural bridge, more than 100 feet long and 10-20 feet wide, is the largest natural bridge in the state. It was formed millions of years ago after an inland sea drained away, exposing the rock to the forces of erosion. While a deep cave-like recess was forming, erosion was working back behind the overhanging ledge, eventually creating the wonder that we see today. In the 1840's, the bridge became a popular stop for tourists on the canal boats that ran between Lancaster and Logan. The loop trail through the preserve is about 1-3/4 miles long.

4. *Route Note:*
   Make a right turn at the end of Starr Route Rd., then right on 678.

5. *Cantwell Cliffs*
   A shelter house, water, and latrines are found here. The hiking trails begin at the shelterhouse.

6. *Rock House*
   The Rock House is found about 5-10 minutes down the trail from the picnic area. This vast Gothic hall, complete with pillars and portals, looks over a beautiful valley below.

7. Conkle's Hollow

One of the most striking nature preserves in Ohio, the grand gorge that is Conkle's Hollow offers us a lesson in persistence. It was not the rushing forces of glacial outwash that created this masterpiece, but rather the steady gentle flow of a stream over thousands of years that sculpted this wonderful gorge. It is an easy 1/2 mile walk along the gorge trail to the waterfall, or take the more challenging Rim Trail (2 mile loop) to learn the origin of the term gorge-ous!

8. Old Man's Cave State Park

One of Ohio's best known natural features, Old Man's Cave is found about 700 feet down the trail from the visitor's center. The center offers historical exhibits of the area. Camping, picnicking, and miles of hiking trails are offered here.

9. Cedar Falls

One cannot help but feel the mystery here, as did the Indians in days gone by. The falls are so named because the settlers mistook the hemlock trees for cedars. The visitor will note the deep grooves and potholes created by the stream cascading over the Blackhand sandstone. Picnic areas and latrines are provided here.

10. Ash Cave

Ash Cave derived its name from the thousands of bushels of ashes found here by the settlers. The ashes were attributed to the numerous tribal fires held here over the years by the Indians. In the 1800's, the cave served as a meeting place that could seat hundreds of people in the huge recess, and the rock overhang provided excellent acoustics. The 90 foot high waterfall is the focal point of the 700 foot horseshoe that forms ash cave, the largest such recess in Ohio. The walk to the falls is an easy stroll along a paved trail, making it accessible for handicapped visitors. Picnic facilities are available here.

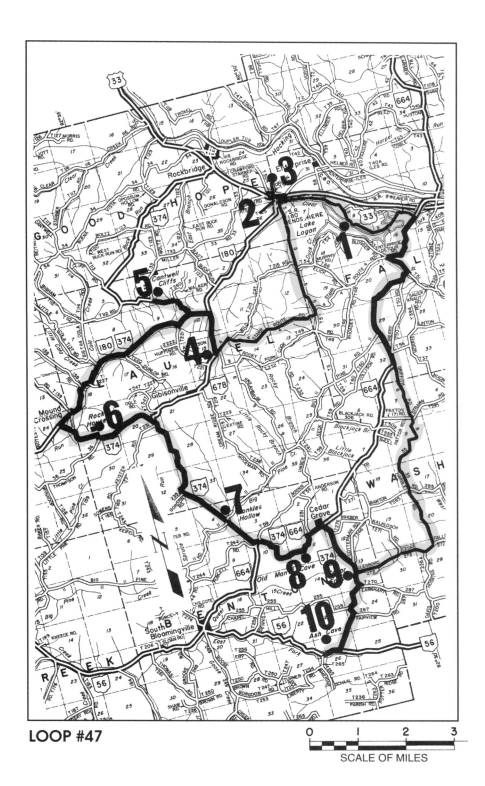

LOOP #47

0   1   2   3

SCALE OF MILES

LOOP #48

Length: 52 miles

Terrain: Generally flat to rolling; few steep hills

County: Ross

Paint Valley Pilgrimage

Historic and beautiful Ross County is the setting of this 52 mile loop through the majestic valley of Paint Creek. The traveler will meander along winding roads that follow sparkling streams and cascades, pass through a beautiful covered bridge, visit two unique burial grounds, and, if one is without fear of the dentist, stop at a museum of dentistry. A community that we believe bears the most unusual name in Ohio is also found along this loop.

Paint Valley, nestled between the hills and knobs that are characteristic of Ross County, was the home of not only some of the earliest and most illustrious Ohio settlers, but was also the home of a mysterious prehistoric people. The Hopewells are known to us today as the ancient builders of the mounds and earthworks that baffled the early pioneers. The centerpiece of this tour is Seip Mound, a huge burial mound and complex constructed by the Hopewell Indians about 2,000 years ago. One of the most impressive of the Hopewell mounds, Seip Mound anchors a 121 acre burial complex. Much of the site has been obliterated by cultivation, but the large mound has survived.

Excavation of Seip Mound, which measures 250 feet in length, 150 feet in width, and is 30 feet high, revealed 122 ancient burials and a number of artifacts, including copper breast plates, grizzly bear teeth with inlaid pearls, mica ornaments, effigy pipes, pottery and projectile points. The contents of the mound indicate that death and burial was a major focus of the Hopewll culture. It is believed that Seip Mound may have been the burial place of the rulers and kings of this prehistoric civilization.

Near the mound, archeologists discovered some 200 holes for posts that supported the framework of Hopewell houses. New posts have been placed in the holes to allow visitors to mentally reconstruct part of the Hopewell village of Paint Valley.

After our stop at Seip Mound, we travel a short distance to another unusual burial ground, this one an American pioneer cemetery, to observe another custom. The cemetery, surrounded by a four foot high stone wall, contains about a dozen graves within its confines. As is the custom in our culture, the graves of war veterans are indicated by special markers. This particular cemetery is the resting place of Christian Platter, a Revolutionary War veteran, as well as veterans of the Civil War.

Following a tour through Bainbridge and along a scenic section of Paint Creek, we invite the traveler to enjoy a picnic and swim at Paint Creek State Park.

POINTS OF INTEREST:

1. **Paint Creek State Park**
   The tour begins at Paint Creek State Park. Camping, hiking, and swimming are available at the park.

2. **Buckskin Covered Bridge**
   This covered bridge, located at the western edge of South Salem, was built over Buckskin Creek in 1873. It is a Smith truss type bridge.

3. **South Salem**
   The impressive brick church on the right as you pass through town is the Presbyterian Church, built in 1855.

4. **Route Note:**
   Use caution on Route 50. You will turn right from Rt. 50 onto the Blain Highway.

5. **Knockemstiff, Ohio**
   This tiny community bears one of the more unusual names in a state that abounds in them. According to local legend, the name resulted from a fight between two women over a man. One of the women told the other, "I'll knock you stiff!", and that became the basis for the town name. The only indication of the town's name is found on the market sign at the edge of town. Efforts to erect official town signs have met with resistance, as some residents fear it would be a less than hospitable welcome to those entering town.

6. *Seip Mound*

Picnic tables, restrooms, and historical displays are available at this historic site. Open year-round, no charge.

7. *Pioneer Cemetery*

This unusual walled cemetery contains about a dozen graves within its confines, including that of Christian Platter, a veteran of the Revolutionary War.

8. *Bainbridge, Ohio*

Bainbridge is proud to be the "cradle of dentistry," and a museum of dentistry is located at 207 W. Main St. in the building that housed the first dental school in America. The traveler passing through town will notice a number of beautiful old buildings that grace the community. Bainbridge was founded by Nathaniel Massie, and it was expected that it would become the county seat of Massie county, a county that was never formed.

9. *Paint Creek Lake*

This Army Corps of Engineering site offers picnic tables, benches, and hiking trails.

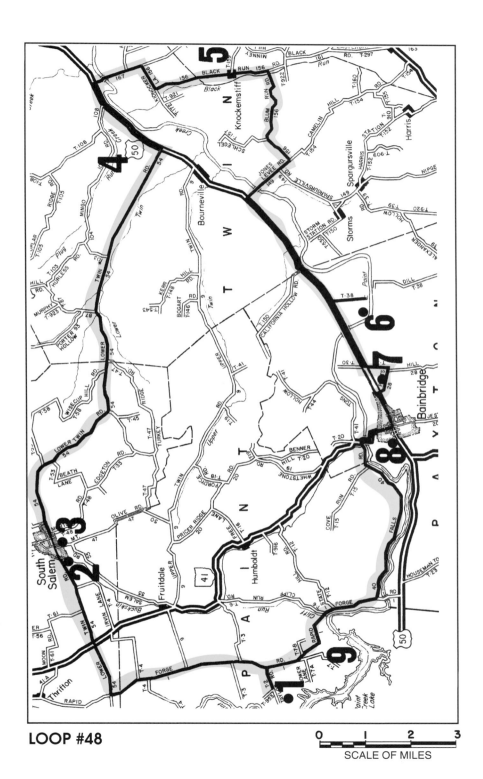

LOOP #48

0   1   2   3

SCALE OF MILES

LOOP #49

Length: 40 miles

Terrain: Rolling to hilly

County: Perry/Fairfield

Perry Pride

This loop along the ridges and valleys of Perry County takes the traveler along scenic roads to visit the birthplaces of two national heroes. Although both were American, one is a national hero to another country. Along the way is the oldest Catholic church in Ohio and a "haunted cemetery" that has given rise to one of southern Ohio's favorite ghost stories, as well as the grave of a fugitive slave who inspired the nation.

While it may be safely presumed that relatively few Ohioans know of Januarius Aloysius MacGahan, who now rests in a cemetery in New Lexington, it has been written that "the Bulgarians heard the voice of God in the burning words of MacGahan's descriptive writings, and hailed him as the Messiah of their race." MacGahan left his Perry County home as a young man to embark on a series of great adventures that eventually helped change the map of Europe. In 1876, he accepted an assignment as a war correspondent to verify atrocities against the Bulgarians. His descriptive accounts of these horrors opened the door for the Russians to intervene, and when MacGahan rode across the Danube with a Russian force of 100,000 men, he was hailed as the "liberator of Bulgaria." MacGahan died in Constantinople after the war at the age of 33, and his body was returned to America. His grave has been a shrine to pilgrims from Bulgaria who journey to the small Ohio town to pay homage to one of the greatest figures in their history.

From New Lexington we travel along scenic roads to Somerset, the birthplace and home of one of America's better known heroes, General Phil Sheridan. "Up from the South at the break of day, bringing to Winchester fresh dismay," began the popular poem about the Union's greatest cavalry leader. The diminutive Sheridan was called "Little Phil" by his admiring troops, who were inspired by his courage. In tribute to his preference to lead from the front, it was said of Sheridan that "he saw the backs of more rebels than any other federal general." In 1865, he made a daring dash through the Shenandoah Valley, hot on the heels of the retreating forces of Robert E. Lee. Seeing the true condition of the Confederate forces, he sent a dispatch to Grant that read, "Hurry up the troops; Lee must surrender if closely pressed, I am sure of it." Grant hurried up the troops, and the war was over.

There is another hero of the Civil War era that is buried along this loop, but this hero never fired a shot. Rather it was a song about his tragic plight that stirred the emotions of the country and enticed many slaves to flee to the north. Joe Selby, a fugitive slave, was on his way to Canada to purchase freedom for his Georgia sweetheart, Nelly Gray. Mr. Selby's desperate flight across Ohio ended in tragedy when he died at the home of the Hanby family in Rushville. On his deathbed he spoke of his darling, Nelly Gray. Benjamin Hanby wrote the famous song "Darling Nelly Gray" to commemorate Joe Selby's tragedy, and the song was sung around Union campfires during the Civil War.

Following a stop at Joe Selby's grave in Rushville, the loop follows scenic roads back to New Lexington.

POINTS OF INTEREST:

1. **New Lexington, Ohio**
   The loop begins in the town of New Lexington, Perry County's seat. A city park with picnic tables is located at the end of Orchard St. off S.R. 13. Follow S.R. 13 North out of town.

2. **St. Joseph's Church and Priory**
   As you travel along Old Somerset Road you will see the spires of the first Catholic church in Ohio looming ahead. This peaceful spot was the site that Dominican fathers selected for a humble log church in 1818. That first church was the result of the missionary work of Father Fenwick, who became Ohio's first Roman Catholic bishop.

3. **Sheridan Home**
   Situated just inside the town limits on the south edge of Somerset, this steamboat Gothic frame dwelling called "Sheridan Grove" was built by General Sheridan for his parents in 1859. On these grounds the young Sheridan listened to William Henry Harrison deliver a campaign speech in 1840. A historical marker is found on the north side of the grounds.

4. Somerset Square

In the center of the town square is the striking figure of General Sheridan mounted upon his horse, seemingly ready to mount a charge against the Confederates. The old county courthouse on the square serves as a reminder that Somerset once served as Perry County's seat.

5. Otterbein Cemetery

This old cemetery is the setting of one of southern Ohio's favorite "ghost stories." Around 1844, James Henry was seeing two young ladies, unable to decide between the two. He fell asleep in his buggy one night and his horse took him to the home of Mary, and he decided this was a sign to marry her. Soon after the marriage she became ill and died. While Mr. Henry was at the cemetery one day, his other girlfriend came by and they struck up a romance. They were soon married. One day shortly after the marriage, his new wife found his body lying face down in the barn behind his first wife's horse. When she rolled him over, she saw the imprint of a horseshoe in his face. It is said that on foggy nights you can hear the hoof beats of Mr. Henry and his first wife riding their horses down Otterbein Road. And on the gravestone of Mary Henry, located in the far corner of the cemetery, is the mysterious imprint of a bloody horseshoe.

6. Rushville, Ohio

This quaint village is the birthplace of Benjamin Hanby, composer of "Darling Nelly Gray."

7. Rushville Cemetery

The grave of Joe Selby is found along the back row of the cemetery, attended by an American flag and a veteran's marker from the Civil War.

8. New Lexington Cemetery

After entering New Lexington on C.R. 57 (Brown St.), continue to the railroad tracks. Just before crossing them, make a double right turn at State up the hill to the end of Swigart St. The grave of MacGahan, marked by his bust, is located on the left side of the center boulevard in the cemetery. After visiting the cemetery, continue up the hill on Brown St. to see the courthouse and a statue of MacGahan at the intersection of Brown and S.R. 13.

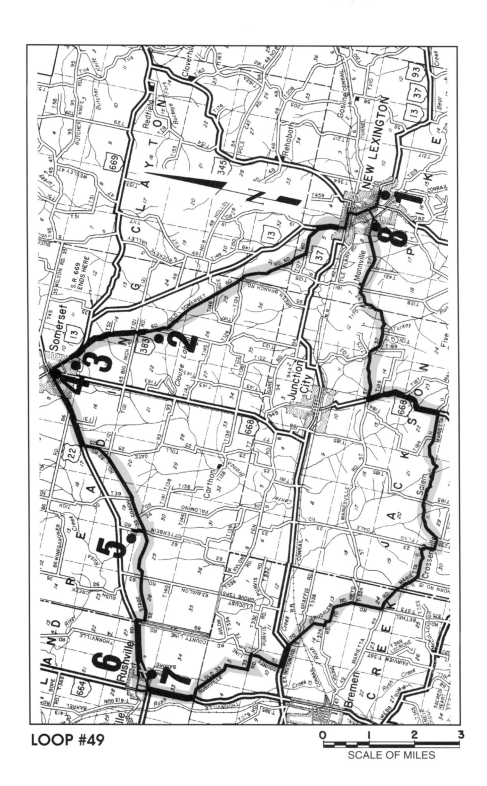

LOOP #49

0   1   2   3

SCALE OF MILES

LOOP # 50

Length: 56 miles

Terrain: Rolling to hilly

County: Muskingum

One for the Road

No tour book of Ohio's back roads would be complete without a tour that pays homage to Ohio's, and the nation's, most famous road. The National Road, a one-time mud pike that cleared the way for coast to coast superhighways, is the centerpiece of this tour from Blue Rock State Park through the rolling hills of Muskingum County. On the way to the National Road we will wind through scenic valleys and along spectacular ridges, stopping to visit an old canal lock and a covered bridge before joining the "Old Pike" and a visit to the National Road Museum. Along the short stretch of today's U.S. 40 that we will travel are found the old mile markers that kept the travelers of a century and a half ago informed of their often painfully slow progress, a charming brick section of the road that is now by-passed, a "road town" that served the travelers, a marker to the first fatality along the road, and a trip across one of the road's most popular curiosities, an S-bridge.

Following the Revolutionary War, George Washington realized that it may have been easier to win the Ohio Country than to keep it. Separated from the original states by a mountain barrier, the west was susceptible to both Spanish and English influence. It was imperative that some means of tying the western territory to the United States be developed. The idea of a road from Cumberland, Maryland to Wheeling on the Ohio River, and eventually into Illinois, was formally signed into law by President Jefferson in 1806, and in 1811 work began at Cumberland on the first federally funded road in America. The road reached Wheeling in 1818, and stood poised ready to cross the Ohio River. After funding disputes delayed the enterprise, a ground-breaking ceremony was held on July 4, 1825 in St. Clairsville. At last, the hard work of road building in Ohio could commence.

Road building in the wilderness was a slow process. A swath 66 feet wide had to be cleared of trees and brush, using only hand tools and teams of oxen. Then, a 32 foot wide road bed made of layers of crushed stone was built. It took fifteen years to build the road across Ohio. As soon as the workers finished a section, it would be filled with sheep, hogs, cattle, geese, and turkeys on the way to market, making the road look like a Noah's Ark. Conestoga wagons, the freight haulers of the day, rumbled over the road, their burly drivers smoking the cigars that became know as "stogies." Inns appeared along the road, some for the more genteel traveler, others little more than a roof over the head.

In the 1850's, the railroad replaced the National Road as the chief means of hauling freight and passengers, and the road languished. It was the bicycling craze of the 1880's that revived the road, and the coming of the automobile before World War I gave it added life. In 1925, the National Road was designated as U.S. 40. Today, U.S. 40 is a sleek modern road, but carries less traffic than one would suppose, for just yards away rushes its own 1960's replacement, Interstate 70.

Following your trek along the National Road, you will loop back over good roads to a picnic at Blue Rock State Park, having earned the distinguished title "Roads Scholar."

POINTS OF INTEREST:

1. **Blue Rock State Park**
   Named for the color of the shale along the Muskingum River, this state park offers camping, swimming, hiking, and picnicking.

2. **Lock 9**
   Located at Philo, this lock is part of the Muskingum River Improvement, a series of dams and locks built in the 1840's to "canalize" the river and link it to the Ohio & Erie Canal. To view the lock, park on the near side of the river in the lot on Water St. and walk across the bridge. To leave Duncan Falls, turn right on Mill St.

3. **Route Note**
   Beginning with Wolf Run Rd., the loop follows roads of lesser quality (gravel or intermittent pavement) for about three miles. After enduring this section, the remainder of the loop is over good roads. The traveler is compensated with scenic views from the ridge tops.

4. **Salt Creek Covered Bridge**
   This Warren truss type bridge was built in 1876 by Thomas Fisher, bypassed in 1953, and is now owned by the Southern Ohio Covered Bridge Association, a group dedicated to educating

the public about these bridges. To join and receive a newsletter, contact SOCBA at 3155 Whitehead Rd., Columbus, OH 43204.

5. **U.S. 40**

Follow U.S. 40, formerly the National Road, as it passes pottery outlets and curves beneath Interstate 70, its successor.

6. **National Road Museum**

The museum offers a fascinating look at the history of the National Road through the use of a 136 foot diorama and other displays. Zane Grey, an Ohio native, and the Ohio pottery industry are also commemorated at the museum. Open daily May-Sept.; Weds.-Sun. Mar., Apr., Oct., and Nov. Admission charge.

7. **Brick Road**

Leave Rt. 40 to rejoin the original road. This stretch of brick road marks the path of the National Road before it was superseded by U.S. 40. The road was bricked in the years just prior to World War I and served to upgrade the nation's military capability.

8. **Norwich, Ohio**

As you follow the National Road through Norwich, you will pass the Old Stone House, built from 1828-36. The inn was completed at a cost of $500, and is on the National Register of Historic Places. Privately owned, it now serves as a nursery and garden center.

9. **First Traffic Accident Marker**

Located on the north side of the street at the far edge of town, this marker is inscribed: "In memory of Christopher Baldwin, Librarian of the American Antiquarian Society, Worcester, Mass. Killed on this curve August 20, 1835 by the overturning of a stage coach, this being the first traffic accident on record in this state."

10. **S-Bridge**

This sturdy stone bridge was built around 1830, and has served as a source of awe and wonder ever since then. The massive stone bridges along the road were a great contrast to the muddy road they carried across streams, and the S-bridge added myth and mystery. Some maintain the design was to avoid large trees in the stream bed, while others hold that they served to stop runaway horses. Perhaps the most colorful story relates that the S-bridge was conceived in a tavern when a stonemason boasted that he could build any bridge, and a designer handed him a paper with an S on it, saying "There! Build that one!" With our apologies, the design is actually a practical one: the center of the S is the actual span across an angled stream, and the end portions are the approaches.

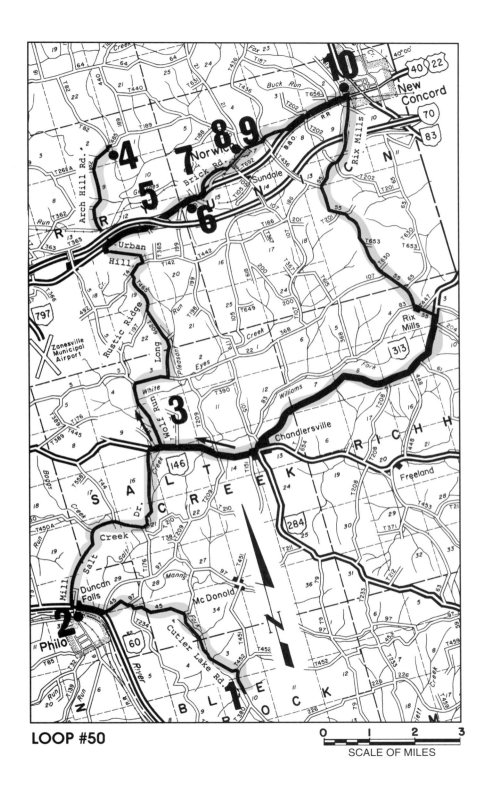

LOOP #50

0   1   2   3

SCALE OF MILES

APPENDIX A
State Parks/Camping in the Slow Lane

Many loops in this book begin at state parks. The following list is for the convenience of those who wish to combine a visit to an Ohio State Park with a tour. A (c) following the park name indicates that camping is available. In several instances, more than one loop originates at a state park where camping is available, providing the option of taking two tours without having to break camp.

STATE PARK:	LOOP NUMBER:
Alum Creek (c)	6
A.W. Marion (c) (2)	7, 8
Beaver Creek (c)	44
Blue Rock (c)	50
Cowan Lake (c)	22
Crane Creek	27
Grand Lake St. Marys (c) (2)	*32, 33, 34
Guilford Lake (c)	43
Harrison Lake (c)	30
Hueston Woods (c) (2)	16, 17
Independence Dam (c)	29
John Bryan (c)	19
Kelleys Island (c)	31
Kiser Lake (c) (2)	3, 4
Lake Alma (c)	46
Lake Logan (c)	47
Lake Loramie (c) (2)	11, 12
Malabar Farm	39
Mohican (c)	39
Paint Creek (c)	48
Rocky Fork (c)	45
Van Buren (c) (2)	25, 26

*Loop 32 originates a considerable distance from the campground at this state park.

For additional information on Ohio's parks, contact the Ohio Department of Natural Resources, Division of Parks and Recreation, Fountain Square, Columbus, OH 43229.

APPENDIX B
Covered Bridges of the Slow Lane

Thirty-five covered bridges are described and plotted on the maps in this book. For the convenience of "bridgers", this appendix lists them in numerical order by loop number. The second number refers to the point of interest number on the loop.

NAME:	NUMBER:
Little Darby Covered Bridge	01-02
Reed Covered Bridge	01-06
Chambers Covered Bridge	06-04
Rock Mill Covered Bridge	09-02
Christman Covered Bridge	14-04
Geeting Covered Bridge	14-13
Roberts Covered Bridge	14-15
Harshman Covered Bridge	16-04
Brubaker Covered Bridge	18-07
Grinnell Covered Bridge	19-03
Stevenson Road Covered Bridge	19-05
Charleton Mill Covered Bridge	19-08
Governor Bebb Preserve Covered Bridge	20-01
Martinsville Covered Bridge	22-02
Brown Covered Bridge	23-05
Newhope Covered Bridge	23-07
Mull Covered Bridge	24-04
Parker Covered Bridge	28-13
Everett Covered Bridge	41-03
Doyle Road Covered Bridge	42-02
Olin Covered Bridge	42-03
Benetka Road Covered Bridge	42-04
State Road Covered Bridge	42-06
Root Road Covered Bridge	42-08
Graham Road Covered Bridge	42-09
Caine Road Covered Bridge	42-10
South Denmark Covered Bridge	42-11
Teegarden Covered Bridge	43-02
Miller Covered Bridge	43-03
Thomas Malone Covered Bridge	44-04
Church Hill Road Covered Bridge	44-07
Buckeye Furnace Covered Bridge	46-03
Byer Covered Bridge	46-07
Buckskin Covered Bridge	48-02
Salt Creek Covered Bridge	50-04

INDEX

The numbers used in the index refer to the loop number and point of interest number. For example, to locate 24-07, refer to loop #24, then find #7 in the points of interest for that loop. In many cases, additional information on the points of interest is found in the loop narrative.

222

223

225

—U—

—V—

—W—

—X—

—Y—

—Z—